ADMAN

MORRIS
HITE'S
METHODS
FOR
WINNING
THE
AD GAME

ADMAN

MORRIS HITE'S METHODS FOR WINNING THE AD GAME

by

RUSS PATE

E-HEART PRESS, INC. DALLAS, TEXAS

Library of Congress Cataloging-in-Publication Data

Pate, Russ.
Adman: Morris Hite's methods for winning the ad game/by Russ Pate.
p. cm.
ISBN 0-935014-12-8 : $19.95
1. Hite, Morris. 2. Advertising—United States—Biography. 3. Marketing—United States—Biography. I. Title.
HF5810.H5P38 1988
659.1'092'4—dc19 [B] 88-16249 CIP

E-Heart Press, Inc.
3700 Mockingbird Lane
Dallas, Texas 75205

Dedication

This book is dedicated to three special women:

Caroline Hite Edens

Rebecca Smith Pate

Mary Katheryn Pate Callahan

Acknowledgments

So many people to thank, so little time to do it. Briefly:

Thanks to Lucille Enix, for her sustained support and encouragement and invaluable editorial advice;

Thanks to Fran Vick and E-Heart Press for believing enough in the idea to take the risk;

Thanks to the family and friends of Morris Hite for being so accessible and eager to help with the research;

Thanks to the executives at Tracy-Locke, M/A/R/C and Point Communications for opening the files;

Thanks to Nora Dodson and Bill Neale for giving this book its look and feel;

Thanks to Becky Pate for sharing me with an Apple Computer;

Finally, thanks to my friends and colleagues at *ADWEEK* magazine, who've taught me that the past seven-plus years writing about advertising has been time well spent.

Contents

Foreword

"Tracy-Locke is looking for an account executive. Why don't you call Morris Hite and come back to Dallas."

I didn't know Morris at the time, but for a native Texan working in New York it was an appealing suggestion. I spent the next 18 years working and playing alongside the man this book is about. I witnessed and shared in much of what you are about to read. Morris was the consummate advertising man.

In supermarkets where Doritos brand tortilla chips, Borden's milk, Mrs Baird's bread and Imperial sugar are sold, "space to sales" was the marketing tactic for a leading brand to get its share of the precious space allotted to the category. In department stores that was not a familiar strategy. But Morris knew that if Haggar slacks could obtain their share of space based on their share of sales, they could increase the store's and Haggar's sales. And that would produce more profit for both.

Morris Hite had applied his experience in food products to a soft goods product in a different type retail outlet. That was what Morris called "idea hunting." Idea hunting meant constantly looking for ways to help the agency's clients build their business and finding new ways to sell more, increase brand share, increase profits.

This book is packed with insights on what a good advertising agency account person should be and do. It is also filled with the philosophies and anecdotes of a man who had no peers as an account man. Morris Hite built an agency by building his clients' businesses.

I first met Morris on a Saturday morning when I returned to Dallas for the interview with Tracy-Locke. That night he and Stewart Mitchell and their wives took me to dinner after a full day in the agency. Sunday I was offered the job. I later learned those long weekend interviews were referred to as the "alcohol test."

The last time I saw Morris was at the Byron Nelson Golf Classic, the day before he was killed in an automobile accident. During the years in between he was my boss, my mentor and my friend. And he never changed from the way he had been that first Saturday morning.

His was the classic Horatio Alger story and he was appropriately the recipient of the award in 1980. From a broken home in Oklahoma, he was raised by grandparents. He left high school after the 10th grade to earn a living. He promoted movies at a local theatre, sold oil leases and real estate by mail and sold himself to an advertising agency in Dallas.

When Morris Hite joined Tracy-Locke as an account executive, he went about the job with a single-minded purpose—building the client's business. He knew the value of advertising in selling a product. He knew instinctively that the message had to communicate what the customer would be interested in, not just what a client wanted to say.

Morris was more committed to the client's business than to the client. He told them what they needed to hear, not what they wanted to hear. He demonstrated his point with facts and clarity. No three syllable words when one syllable would do.

He taught others what a good account person had to be. But he couldn't make you a great account man. "That has to come from within yourself," he believed. "You have to eat and sleep your client's business. Sweat his problems before he does. Hunt for ideas in his plant, with his salesmen, with his customers and with his consumers. Look for his competitors' weaknesses and develop a plan to take advantage of them."

Advertising was not a game to Morris, but he loved to

play. He hated to lose and worked at winning. Whether in a new business pitch or on a golf course, he played the best he could play. And he inspired that in those around him.

Morris' enthusiasm was contagious. He enjoyed everything he did and it was an experience to share it with him. He jumped right into the middle of the action. When Glenn Advertising in Dallas (now BJK&E) challenged Tracy-Locke to a softball game, Morris was out of town and returned after the game started. He came directly from the airport, took off his coat and tie and asked if he could play catcher. He had more hustle than the young account executive he relieved. And he drank the most Pearl beer after the game to celebrate our winning.

At a surprise party on Morris' 65th birthday everyone in the agency contributed to roasting him. He loved every jibe and had an immediate retort that invariably was an equalizer. He could laugh louder at himself than anyone. Some of the greatest nights of my life were with groups of people in the agency telling stories and drinking scotch with Hite.

Morris believed in employees owning stock in Tracy-Locke. He felt you had a vested interest in the company's performance and it was better to invest in a company you could impact on than one you couldn't. From the time I was offered my first share of Tracy-Locke stock, I bought every share I could. I paid more to the bank for stock than I paid on my mortgage because it was *my* company.

Morris Hite embodied what clients want from their agencies—a fervent commitment to help build their business. He knew the value of advertising in building and maintaining a brand's sales growth and market share. He understood marketing intuitively and instinctively because he constantly worked at knowing products and consumers. His passion for the business was pervasive in the agency and with clients.

Morris could read a Nielsen report, but he said he

learned a lot more talking to store managers and buyers. He could write a strategy statement, but more often than not it was so clear he could write the headline as well. And he often did.

To those who knew Morris Hite he was a legend in his own time. Everyone in this business would have benefited from the privilege of knowing and working with him.

Norman W. Campbell
Chairman and Chief Executive Officer
BBDO Worldwide Inc.

INTRODUCTION

"THE SON OF A BITCH FROM THE HOME OFFICE WITH SPECIAL PRICES."—MORRIS HITE

Consider for a moment the ad agency account person: He or she faces the awesome task of seeing that a client's needs get met. That the agency's finished products—TV commercials, print ads or any other persuasive selling messages—have strategic objectives. That the finished products are completed on schedule and within budget. That regardless of whether the finished product is a 30-second TV commercial for a local market in Kalamazoo or Kissimmee or a four-color ad in a national newsweekly magazine in New York, time or space has been reserved. And that the media outlet receives the finished product within a specified deadline and in good working order.

The ad agency account person duly records each step of the process, from the formation of marketing objectives (the plan) to the creation of a selling message (the ad), in documents known as conference reports. The ad agency account person makes sure that copies of conference reports get circulated to anyone on the agency's or client's payroll who has anything whatsoever to do with the account. Or anyone who ever will, regardless of how remote the chance.

There's an acronym for these reports: CYA. As in Cover Your Ass memos. Should a breakdown in the advertising process occur, the applicable rule of thumb is "Blame it on them before they can blame it on you." Paranoia runs deep.

Despite shouldering such a major responsibility as

keeping the client satisfied—perhaps because of it—the ad agency account person has become the ad industry's butt-of-the-joke. The patsy. The stooge. The object of malice and scorn.

The ad agency account person often gets stereotyped as a wishy-washy, mealy-mouthed brown-noser. A yes-man or yes-woman. Someone utterly lacking in personal convictions, reluctant to take a stand without first considering his client's position on the issue. A lackey. A toady. Or worse.

Advertising account people also get labeled as slick, glib and fatuous, smooth-talkers who could charm the rattle off a rattlesnake or sell ice cubes to Eskimos. They are the spiritual descendants of the snake-oil salesman and the faith-healer. The Dr. Feelgoods.

Unlike the ad men and women who work on the creative side—the industry's darlings, hailed for their elegant choice of imagery or turn of phrase and canonized for their imagination and vision—ad agency account people remain unknown and unappreciated. Creative people get phone calls from publishers wanting to see manuscripts or meeting planners seeking seminar participants; account people get calls from the client ad manager, who's bent out of shape because his boss, the vice president of marketing, has just been reamed out by the executive vice president. And that's because the big guy upstairs is *really* pissed.

Advertising creatives use a favorite term of derision for account people: *Suits*. They tag the most ineffectual account people as *Empty Suits*. The concept derives from the observable preference account people have for attire by Brooks Brothers or The Corporate Woman. Clothing happens to be one of the many lines of demarcation between agency account people and creatives, who tend to dress out of the L.L. Bean catalog, except for the Reebok sneakers. (Office decor, facial hair, political persuasion and ingestion of chemical substances being other points of difference.)

It's of small consolation that the account person tends to be the most handsomely compensated employee in the agency. Higher paid on average than the artists and copywriters who create the ads, higher paid than the media specialists who plan where and when the ads will appear, higher paid than the researchers who analyze the market to determine the strategic objectives for the ad campaign. Higher paid on average than everyone, in fact, but the agency principal, who has his name on the company stationery and his imported sports car in the reserved parking space.

Money can't buy respect for an ad agency account person, but it can buy a three-martini lunch. That's something for which the advertising world is renowned. And money can also buy a sprawling home in the suburbs, far away from those creative hotshots who want to *experience* the pulse of city life.

So there.

The story of Morris Hite, a principal figure in the evolution of advertising in the Southwest, makes a strong counterpoint to the stereotype of the ineffective and ineffectual agency account person. Hite's brand of advertising account service can be described as take-charge, assertive or hands-on. Instead of taking orders from his advertising clients, he *led* their selling efforts.

No one ever called Morris Hite wishy-washy or mealy-mouthed. Nor did anyone ever describe him as slick or glib. Long on substance and short on style, Hite dealt with people the only way he knew how: directly and fairly. He spoke to everyone—clients, prospects, or employees—in a frank, straightforward manner. He didn't finesse anyone. Or b.s. them.

The longtime president and chief executive officer at Tracy-Locke Co. in Dallas, Morris Hite employed a perspective on advertising gleaned from having worked both as an advertising creative and account man. In the years before he joined Tracy-Locke, Hite ran his own small ad agency and gained first-hand experience in everything from soliciting clients to creating their ads to collecting the money they owed him for services rendered. Which is to say, he didn't underestimate the role of creativity in advertising.

Yet Morris Hite's experiences taught him that the most critical function in advertising belongs to the agency account person. With him or her rests the ultimate responsibility to see that advertising performs its principal purpose: helping to sell a client's goods or services.

Morris Hite's career in advertising began in the late 1920s and stretched to the early 1980s, a span of nearly six decades. He made his living in advertising when the dominant media were print (newspapers, magazines, direct mail) and when the dominant media were broadcast (television, radio). He absorbed the nuances of each form of communications. As the business changed, so did he.

But Hite held steadfastly to a philosophy of keeping the business simple. Even as the age of computers and M.B.A.s engulfed him, he never lost sight of the fact that the most effective selling messages are simple, direct and based on a sound strategy or rationale.

At the time of his death in a traffic accident on May 1, 1983, Morris Hite engaged himself principally with building a communications conglomerate called Allcom. He was 72 years old. He planned to extend his career by teaching his advertising methods to a new generation of adpeople.

Hite's skill as an agency account person can be attributed in part to the fact he never acted as an arm's-length consultant, applying cookie-cutter solutions to customers' problems. Nor did he tell his clients what he thought they wanted to hear. Hite refused to recommend solutions until he fully understood a client's problem. That took digging.

Digging kept Hite in the field assimilating facts. He broke down the selling process, analyzing each of the incremental steps between when a product came out of a manufacturing line until it reached the ultimate consumer. He interviewed people at every step, from the distributor and wholesaler to the retailer moving the goods.

Hite buttonholed shoppers and found out the reasons behind their brand loyalty and buying patterns long before marketing research became such a fundamental aspect of selling. He came to know and understand the American grocery shopper probably as well as anyone who ever worked in advertising. That should come as no surprise when you consider that his primary accounts, some of which he handled more than 40 years, included dairy products (Borden), bakery products (Mrs Baird's Bread), snack foods (Frito-Lay), coffee (Maryland Club) and beer (Regal, Pearl).

Hite also possessed people skills, a critical element for any advertising account person. Some clients turned to Morris for answers on problems outside of the marketing realm. One of his clients, Imperial Sugar, elected Hite to its board of directors, a rare accolade for an advertising man.

In addition to his advertising enterprises, Hite volunteered his time and his agency's services to a large number of civic causes that hastened the development of Dallas as a city of international scope. Meanwhile, he helped raise a family of five children, no little feat in itself.

All of which left precious little time for Morris Hite to play Mr. Big-Shot. Long after he made his first million dollars in advertising, and his second and third million in oil and real estate, Hite remained just plain Morris. Someone who would listen to your problems and offer advice. Someone you could count on in a pinch. Your basic straightshooter, a guy without an ounce of pretentiousness in his being. A down-to-earth adman.

Some of the most recognizable names in the history of advertising—David Ogilvy, Bill Bernbach, Leo Burnett—shared a background in creativity. Agency bosses with their names on the door (Ogilvy & Mather, Doyle Dane Bernbach, Leo Burnett Co.), they focused less on account service than on the creative product. For them, creativity represented an ad agency's lifeblood.

Morris Hite, by contrast, believed wholeheartedly that the agency account person performs advertising's primary function. The account person's spadework to uncover a client's sales opportunities turns up the fertile ground on which creatives can cultivate their words and images. Hite believed the ability of an account person to isolate and identify sales opportunities—"big ideas" he called them—ultimately determines whether the denim-clad, tennis-shoed creative person succeeds or fails.

Morris Hite's story is one to be read and remembered by all men and women who work in account service. People who walk the point in the advertising wars, who handle the countless details that accompany managing a client's account.

The agency account person needs a role model, too. He or she would be hard-pressed to find a better one than Morris Hite, the account man's champion.

CHAPTER ONE

"THIS IS A SIMPLE BUSINESS. JUST A MATTER OF MAKING SURE THE COMING IN IS MORE THAN THE GOING OUT."—MORRIS HITE

Morris Hite awoke in an antsy mood on Monday, January 7, 1957, after a typically fitful night. Hite had seldom been able to sleep peacefully after sustaining a back injury in World War II that damaged several vertebrae. Lying in bed, he frequently imagined that thousands of tiny pins and needles pricked his back. It hurt.

The adman's sleeping habits—he tossed and turned as much as a short order cook—also reflected the difficulty he had winding down at night. Hite shifted mental gears constantly, racing from this project to that and back again. *Idea-hunting* he called it. He kept a notepad and pencil on the night table by his bed and he'd frequently bolt upright, switch on a lamp and jot down ideas for selling milk, bread, sugar or any of the other products his advertising agency, Tracy-Locke Co., represented.

Hite glanced at his watch: 5:30. Careful not to disturb his wife lying beside him, he slid out of bed and headed for the bathroom shower. Luckily for Caroline Hite, she slept as soundly as her husband did poorly, a fact that allowed Morris to keep a bedside stack of books and magazines and fill many sleepless hours with reading. More idea-hunting.

The pending arrival of January 7, 1957, filled Morris Hite with anticipation throughout the holiday season of 1956. It occupied his thoughts as he escorted his wife to party after holiday party in Dallas, especially since the social scene wasn't exactly Morris's cup of egg nog.

"If I can make it through all these Christmas and New Year's cocktail parties, living another year will be a cinch," joked Hite, who also liked to say, "The next time I get married, I'm going to marry a six-foot-three redhead, so when she sends me to the bar to get her a drink at a cocktail party, I can always find her." He simply didn't care for cocktail chatter; he preferred to talk business.

Thoughts of January 7 didn't disappear altogether even as Morris watched his four children—Lee, Jerry, Sissy and Florence—scamper about opening presents on Christmas morning. Or when he took Caroline dancing at Glen Lakes Country Club on New Year's Eve and kissed her at the midnight hour.

Morris Hite simply couldn't get January 7 out of his mind because it meant too much to his present and future. He planned to assemble his employees at Tracy-Locke that morning and read them the riot act. He knew the time had come to kick ass and take names.

Hite would have no trouble taking a hard-line approach with his admen, either. The skipper of an Army tugboat that saw action in the Pacific toward the end of World War II, Major Morris Hite knew a thing or two about motivating people. Life-or-death situations have a way of teaching a person that.

Hite intended to get his staff working toward a common goal of excellence through a classroom exercise he called the Account Executive's Training School. The first session: January 7. The headmaster: Morris Hite. The class: Tracy-Locke account men.

Hite sensed that some Tracy-Locke account men had developed sloppy work habits. And others didn't know what the hell they were supposed to be doing. If these people couldn't do their jobs properly, then by God Morris Hite would teach them how.

Not that he especially cared for such harsh measures. Hite preferred to lead by example. He might give an individual some guidance or counsel where he sensed a need, and he stood ready to give advice when asked, but generally he preferred to show rather than to tell.

But toward the end of 1956, Morris assessed Tracy-Locke's performance and handed out a failing grade. Hite, who had been with the agency for almost 20 years, roughly the last seven as president, knew that there's no status quo in the advertising world. Either an ad agency moves forward or it goes backward. There's no neutral gear. No idle.

Tracy-Locke had moved forward in 1956, in the sense that billings, the ad industry's term for an agency's revenues, increased 14 percent over 1955 and profits had been the second highest in the agency's 43-year history. Yet Morris could detect a growing complacency, even something of a cavalier spirit, exhibited by his account service staff. Several account executives came to work late, left early and took extended lunches. Even worse, Hite had begun to hear clients grumbling about the level and quality of service on their accounts.

Nothing infuriated him more than poor account service. The mere hint that a Tracy-Locke client didn't receive the type of commitment that he, Morris Hite, had promised them made his blood boil. He could put up with some glitches and botches in the ad business. Those happen all the time. But he'd be goddamned if he'd put up with inattentiveness or indifference on the part of his staff.

By 6:10 a.m., Hite sat at the table in the kitchen, going over the notes he'd prepared for the 7 a.m. showdown. That Hite went to such lengths of preparing a script for his opening remarks, not to mention a course syllabus, showed how serious he felt about the training exercise.

Normally, Hite would have spoken to the staff off-the-cuff. His friendly, folksy delivery invited comparisons with a fellow Oklahoman named Will Rogers. Not that Hite was as funny, of course. But Morris's combination of Okie drawl, self-deprecating wit and an ability to tell a story—embellishing it here or there, naturally—enabled him to keep his audience amused and informed. Tracy-Locke clients loved to hear him talk. Several of them booked Hite year after year as the motivational speaker at their company's annual sales meetings. He had a way of making his audience believe that selling represented man's most noble endeavor on earth.

Morris' musings about the training program had diverted his attention away from *The Dallas Morning News* lying out on the driveway at 6614 Brookshire. On any other Monday morning, Hite would have spent an hour reading the morning paper front to back. The news columns. The advertisements. Everything.

A newshound, and a Republican at that, Hite would have paid particular attention to the news stories about the so-called "Eisenhower Doctrine." Over the previous weekend, President Dwight D. Eisenhower, responding to the threat of Communist intervention in the Middle East, had declared that America would take appropriate action, even military intervention, to thwart any Communist aggression.

But tensions in the Middle East would have to wait because of the tensions at Tracy-Locke. So, too, would the stories on the sports page about the retirements of future Hall-of-Famers Bob Feller and Jackie Robinson. Morris loved baseball, all sports really, almost as much he loved current events. He enjoyed discussing the teams and standings with his uncle, Boone Hite, who lived in a Dallas nursing home, and with his sons, Lee and Jerry.

On any other Monday morning, Morris would have eaten a big breakfast with his family. Caroline fixed a platter of eggs and bacon and the kids washed down their meals with a glassful of milk. Borden's milk, to be sure, because Morris believed in consuming the products his clients sold and Tracy-Locke had handled the Borden account since 1915.

For the same reason of client loyalty, the toast on the Hite table came from Mrs Baird's Bakeries, the sugar in the coffee came from Imperial Sugar Co. and the coffee itself carried the Maryland Club label of Duncan Coffee Co. In the world according to Morris Hite, using a competitors' brand amounted to an act of treason.

But on January 7, 1957, Morris didn't eat breakfast at home. At 6:30, he backed his Oldsmobile out of the driveway and headed to the office. Tracy-Locke occupied space in a two-story building at the intersection of Fairmont and Cedar Springs in the Oak Lawn area near downtown. Hite's 25-minute drive to the office took him south down Preston Rd. past the Dallas neighborhoods of Preston Hollow, University Park and Highland Park, where the old money in Dallas resided.

Driving an automobile amounted to an Achilles' heel for Hite. He couldn't keep his concentration on the road. His mind tended to drift. To a client's marketing strategy. To a new business presentation. To a slogan he thought would work in a new ad campaign.

Once, on a trip to a Champlin Oil sales meeting at a resort in northeastern Oklahoma, Morris took a wrong turn leaving the airport in Tulsa. He drove merrily along, lost in thought. Hite didn't realize his mistake until more than an hour later, when he saw a road sign reading "Welcome to Kansas." The Champlin oilmen roared with delight when Morris, the after-dinner speaker who arrived three hours late for dinner, apologized by telling the story on himself.

On another occasion, Morris borrowed a car from Fred Rowe, a Tracy-Locke vice president, and drove to a new business presentation in Abbeville, Louisiana. Hite began talking with his traveling companion, researcher

Jack Taylor, about a prospect's rice milling operation and became absorbed in the conversation. Suddenly, he felt the car begin to shake, rattle and roll.

"This car's got a pretty bad vibration," said Hite. "We'd better tell Fred about it when we get back, so he can have it checked out."

Morris didn't realize the vibration had to do with his driving along at 90 mph, the gas pedal depressed to the floorboard.

No, Hite's associates didn't embrace the idea of having to ride in a moving vehicle with him. Mostly because he kept one eye on the highway and one eye on the person to whom he spoke. Never mind if that person happened to be sitting in the back seat.

Some Tracy-Locke people genuinely feared for his safety behind the wheel. In the summer of 1982, when Hite headed the campaign for a pivotal City of Dallas bond election, some of his colleagues urged him to let a chauffeur drive him from appointment to appointment. Nonsense, scoffed Morris. He could damn well drive his own car. And drive he did.

Hite's drive to work on January 7, 1957 gave him time to reflect on Tracy-Locke's state of affairs. It galled him to see the agency losing the momentum it had been building since he'd taken charge in 1950.

Hite succeeded one of the agency's co-founders, Raymond P. Locke, as president and principal shareholder. For years, Locke had concentrated his energies, and Tracy-Locke's, on servicing the account of Dr Pepper, the Dallas-based soft drink manufacturer. Locke personally had a hand in coining Dr Pepper's popular slogan, "Drink A Bite To Eat At 10, 2 and 4 O'Clock."

But in 1949, a change in corporate ownership at Dr Pepper brought to an end an affiliation between the client and Tracy-Locke that dated back to 1926. The blow rocked the entire agency, Ray Locke most of all. Locke lost his zest for the business; within a year he'd sold out his interest to a group headed by Hite.

The ad agency graveyard, it should be noted, is full of shops that became too dependent on a single account. Hite, long aware of Tracy-Locke's vulnerability with Dr Pepper, had set out to add a mix of clients—consumer, financial, corporate, business-to-business—to the account roster.

In his seven years as chief executive, Morris had put his personal stamp on the agency. If Tracy-Locke had acquired a reputation as a sweat shop—60-hour weeks were normal, weekend work required—it also had earned the reputation as Texas's most professional ad agency. In no small part because of its straight-shooting boss.

As Morris Hite drove to Tracy-Locke Co. on the morning of January 7, 1957, the business at hand dealt with reality, not reputation. The reality he faced had to do with the poor performance by his Tracy-Locke account men. Morris Hite aimed to fix that. And fast.

CHAPTER TWO

"THE AGENCY'S ACCOUNT EXECUTIVE SHOULD BE ABLE TO STEP INTO THE SALES MANAGER'S SHOES IF THE SALES MANAGER DROPS DEAD TODAY."—MORRIS HITE

At precisely 7 a.m. on January 7, 1957, Morris Hite surveyed his staff of 15 account people, several of whom had been with him since he took over as boss. He searched their faces for signs of the ambition they would need to help him reach his goal of making Tracy-Locke one of the nation's largest and most respected ad agencies.

The account men crowded into Hite's corner office on the second floor included Clay Stephenson, executive vice president and head of the agency's Houston office, and Ken Browning, the head guy in New Orleans. The Dallas contingent included Fred Rowe, the Ivy Leaguer; Bill James, the ex-military man; Newsome Gay, the former Southwest Conference track star; Cecil "Bud" Phillips and Jack Taylor, the research specialists; Paul Rafferty, who handled Haggar slacks; Frank Smith, who handled Champlin Oil; and Gene Thomas, who handled Southern Union Gas.

A smattering of personnel from other disciplines joined the account people. Larry DuPont from broadcast services. Bill Neale from the art department. Bill Muessig from print production.

Hite set the ground rules for his Account Executive's Training School. Over the next 12 weeks everyone would be required to attend a Monday morning training session and complete a homework assignment during the week.

"These meetings are mandatory, gentlemen," said Morris. "The only valid excuses will be a death or funeral, and in either case it had damn well better be your own." He used the word 'gentlemen' as no women were present. Not in Dallas. Not in advertising. Not in the 1950s.

Morris explained that the account men's performance had slipped noticeably, causing him to see a need to go over the basics of the business. The scene suggested how Vince Lombardi started training camps with the NFL champion Green Bay Packers. "This, gentlemen, is a football," said the Green Bay coach.

Morris Hite intended to use his account training school to say, "This, gentlemen, is advertising."

Hite began tapping his foot, an unconscious habit that allowed associates to gauge Morris's mood and intensity. The more wound up he got, the faster he tapped.

"The purpose of this training program is to standardize our methods of account handling at the highest level of effectiveness," he said. "On some of our accounts, we do a fine job of account handling. On other accounts we do a lesser job. The objective is to bring the poorest job of account handling up to our highest standard. If we do that, we will be doing all right.

"It has been a stated policy of this agency that if we can't give an account the best service that we are capable of delivering, then we should not take the account in the first place. There should be no variation in quality of service."

Hite believed that if an ad agency's clients were given the proper account service, their business would grow. He had that much confidence in carefully crafted marketing plans and the advertising campaigns that supported them. He had plenty of first-hand experience with using advertising and marketing programs to boost a company's sales. He also knew that if Tracy-Locke's clients achieved sales increases, then the agency's business would grow as well. Just as surely as night follows day.

Morris outlined the financial goals of the company, among them increasing the amount of contributions to the company's profit-sharing plan and establishing a pension plan.

"Several [of you] have expressed interest in Tracy-Locke stock, but there has been no need to increase capital stock. We haven't built enough volume to require additional operating capital. If we can build volume . . . there will be a reason to expand capital stock and to extend the opportunity of ownership to those people who make the greatest contribution."

"Fundamentally, this program is designed to help everybody make more money," he said. "For each of us to make more money, we must make the agency grow; to make the agency grow, the account executives must do a better job because *no agency is better than its account executives*."

This was the beginning of 1957, still several years before advertising's heralded "creative revolution." During that period, highlighted by the rise of the Bill Bernbachs (Doyle Dane Bernbach), Mary Wellses (Wells, Rich, Greene) and the George Loises (Lois, Papert, Koenig) the conventional wisdom on Madison Avenue changed to *No agency is better than its creative talent*.

Morris Hite never emphasized the creative product. Not in the 1930s and 1940s when he was coming of age in advertising, certainly not in 1957 when he conducted the agency's training school. Not even a decade later when the industry went gaga over creativity.

Not that he discounted its value. He believed that a strategic intent belonged at the core of all effective advertising and the strategic intent, or selling idea, gave consumers a "reason why" to purchase an advertiser's products or services.

"If you have a good selling idea," Morris insisted, "your secretary can write your ad for you."

Within the advertising industry—then and now—some admen consider creativity to be the driving force. They view creative excellence as an end unto itself. A memorable ad, *breakthrough* being the current vogue expression, penetrates a target market's consciousness, drawing attention to a particular product and separating it from its competition in customer awareness, recall and, ultimately, use. Breakthrough advertising registers at an emotional level that not only triggers consumer purchases but creates within customers a deep-seated brand loyalty.

Morris Hite saw the role of creativity not as an end, but as a means. A means by which to help his clients sell, whether the product be milk or eggs, guns or butter. In Hite's view, an ad agency's ultimate aim should be to help customers sell, not to create great advertising.

Having made that point clear, Hite contrasted the role of Tracy-Locke's account executives with those of Young & Rubicam, a prominent New York agency that ranked, then and now, among the industry's largest and most powerful. At Y&R, scoffed Hite, account executives amount to little more than errand boys, kept running back-and-forth to the client's offices by agency management.

"They carry packages to the clients; untie the strings; open them up and let the client look at the ads. They are briefed before they go to the client's office as to what their position will be in regard to the material contained in the packages. They can't roll with the punch. They can't change position. They can't do anything but maintain steadfast on what they are told to deliver to the client. If the client turns the material down, all they can do is to say they are sorry and take it back to the agency for further instructions."

Morris strongly disagreed with that approach. Giving the account service people so little responsibility, asking them in effect to be nothing more than glorified "go-fers" gave them little sense of accomplishment or self-esteem. They felt estranged from the agency's operation, not a real part of it. They didn't add depth to an agency's talent pool because they weren't given a chance to succeed or fail on their own terms. They weren't given a chance to *grow.*

Hite believed building an agency meant finding the best available talent, problem-solvers and action-oriented people, and allowing them to work closely with a client. Make that *insisting* that they work closely with a client.

Hite's foot tapped faster and faster. "An account executive should know the client's business so well that he commands respect in the client's office. He should be able to advise the client on all phases of his advertising, selling and marketing program. He should quarterback the agency's basic thinking. That is the type of account executive we want here at Tracy-Locke."

Hite held up a piece of paper and explained to the staff it was a self-evaluation sheet, a measuring stick that would indicate a person's job performance. "We're going to have each of us fill one of these things out," he said.

But first Morris offered a brief history of Tracy-Locke. "Everybody who represents this company should know something of its background," he said, hoping to instill a sense of company pride.

He quickly recited the agency's past. Formed in Oklahoma City in 1913 as the Southwestern Advertising Co. Moved to Dallas and renamed Tracy-Locke-Dawson in the 1920s. Shifted its focus to New York in the 1930s and ranked among the U.S. ad industry's 25 largest shops. Dissolved its original partnership in the early 1940s and reorganized as Tracy-Locke Co.

"Our philosophy is simple to express but really hard to live by," said Hite. "Simply stated, our philosophy and policy is to do whatever is necessary to get profitable sales increases for our clients.

"Ray Locke used to express it: 'Advertising must pay its way and pay a profit.' By that we mean that if it takes cooperative advertising, on which an agency earns no commission, to sell the goods, then we recommend cooperative advertising. If it takes in-store demonstrations, upon which the agency earns no commission, we recommend in-store demonstrations. The policy is that we must recommend what will sell the goods at a profit to the client."

Hite paused. "You might say you can go broke that way, but you won't because any client will pay for profitable sales. If he's got to pay a fee, he'll pay a fee; he will pay if you do a job; if you show him how to sell more merchandise and make more profit, he'll pay you."

Morris shared a story about being sent out to evaluate the performance of a client's division managers and district managers. "In short the client asked us to tell them how to do a better selling job. And you know what else he said? 'I'm not asking you to do anything for nothing. I know you've got to make a profit.'"

Hite continued, "Our job in advertising is becoming more and more a marketing job. The ad agency is no longer a service operation that writes copy and runs it back and forth to the client waiting for approval. An advertising agency today must understand business and selling well enough to help the client organize his selling force to move merchandise. If the agency and the agency's account men actually know enough about the client's business to help move merchandise, the client will pay for the service."

He reiterated the Tracy-Locke creed: *Do what is necessary to get profitable sales increases for our clients.* "Our policy is to do a good job first and worry about how we get paid later. That attitude may sound altruistic but it's not. It is a practical attitude in business and in your own personal life. I can guarantee you this one thing: that any time an employee of an organization holds his first thought on how he can increase his salary, how he can make more money, he'll be the last man to get a raise.

"The man who thinks first about doing a better job—

who gets up in the morning and goes to work saying to himself How can I do a better job? How can I help my company do a better job? How can I help my client do a better job? How can I help my client sell more merchandise? *He* will be the first man to make more money for himself.

"He'll be getting raises in pay without even thinking about it because he'll be earning more money for his client and his company and the raise just comes automatically. But if you put it just the other way and start figuring what can I do to get a raise? . . . If you start thinking about looking good and saying the right thing instead of worrying about producing . . . you won't get ahead.

"The same rule applies in business," said Hite, his toe tapping furiously. "I don't care whether it's in the advertising agency business, milk business, sugar business—the business that thinks *first* about making money instead of serving its customers is damn near doomed to failure. Or at least mediocrity."

Hite illustrated his point by describing The Borden Co.'s Houston milk plant, which operated on the principle of service first, profits second. "There's the most successful milk business in the United States. But John Luker, the manager, never approached it from the basis of how much money can I make out of the milk business in Houston. He approached it from the standpoint—how good a bottle of milk can I give to the people of Houston and at how low a cost can I sell it to them? How good can I make the milk and how economically can I sell it?

"As his volume grew, instead of letting his profits grow to phenomenal figures, he cut down on his profit spread. Instead of trying to cash in quickly, he cut the spread down and made it impossible for the competition to take business away from him. He wasn't thinking about today's profit—but the percent of market. Holding back the competition.

"Did that policy of service work? When he first started

that operation there were nine major milk companies in Houston . . . today there are only five left. Competing against Borden in Houston they just flat couldn't make it. Borden has 46 percent of the total market *without* home delivery. It's the most fabulous success story in the entire milk business. It was built by selling the best bottle of milk at the lowest possible price. It was built by thinking first of service, second of profits. This plant with the smallest profit spread in the business, makes the largest total profit of any other Borden operation."

Hite drove home the point. The rule of service, first, is fundamental in both personal success and business success. It must be a fundamental in the operation of this agency.

Service meant immersion in the client's business. "We must build our reputation as a marketing agency," Hite stressed. "The account executive must learn the client's business. Every account executive in this room, if the sales manager on his account had a heart attack at high noon today, ought to be able to go over there and do his job. He ought to know the business that well.

"That is a major assignment and it is not something that you can learn in 90 days or even in three years. But, to be a finished account executive, you should be able to do that."

Morris also called for better creativity. Naturally, he placed the onus on his account executives.

"We want our account executives to be creative account executives. We just don't think that great advertising ideas can come from people who are not exposed to the sales problem. Now, a writer may translate an idea into more forceful phrasing, may develop a better word picture or may develop a better vehicle for carrying that thought, but the first basic thought is going to come from a guy who is exposed to the problem . . . who rubs up against it so often and lives it so close that it permeates his subconscious mind."

For Tracy-Locke to become a better creative agency, Morris said, account executives must spend more time idea-hunting.

"The only time you're going to have any ideas that are worth a damn is when you get so full of the problem that at home, when you're sitting around reading *Sports Illustrated* your mind may wander off and you get a sudden flash . . . a thought about your client's problem. It may happen to you when you're shaving, but the only way you're ever going to get those thoughts is by consciously making an effort during some periods of relaxation so that you get your mind to churning on it."

He recommended that his account people study the strategic messages and selling ideas behind them.

"Trace the reasoning behind the ads," he advised. "Why did they say this? Why did they do it? Do you think it's a good campaign or not? Will it really sell any merchandise or is it just another piece of name publicity?" Hite was scornful of ads that didn't sell.

"If you're in the food business, you ought to enjoy going home and studying the *Ladies' Home Journal* and *Good Housekeeping* to see what women are reading about food. You ought to enjoy talking to your wife and your neighbors' wives about their problems in cooking. Train yourself to always be on the alert for an idea.

"The trouble with most of us is that an idea jumps up and bites us and all we do is kick it off because our minds are not open to receive ideas when they come in," he said. "Idea-hunting can be fun if you train yourself during leisure hours to expose yourself to ideas. That is the secret of creativity.

"There are few geniuses in this business," he observed. "The only successful idea-men that I've ever seen are men who are willing to take the time to sit down and give their minds a chance to come up with something."

His discourse on creativity and idea-hunting concluded, Hite turned his attention to what he called "standards" for account executives. He spelled out the basics of acceptable performance.

MORRIS HITE'S TWELVE STANDARDS FOR ACCOUNT EXECUTIVES

1. *Earn your client's respect and friendship.*

"The way you do that is by being a salesman of ideas. Ideas that will solve your client's problems and help his sales grow."

2. *An account executive's primary responsibility is basic planning, creating the client's advertising and merchandising strategy.*

"The account executive is not going to be isolated in his office and be made responsible for the entire job. We want the account executives to use all departments, to call on everybody for help. We don't want one-man thinking. Make it a group effort, but the account man is the quarterback."

3. *Account executives will be required to write an annual plan to each account.*

"It's possible to write a plan and say nothing, but to write a real good plan is the hardest work you've ever done since you've been with this agency. It requires concentration. It requires going out and learning about the client's business. It requires learning things about the client's business that the client doesn't know himself."

4. *Develop the basic thinking of an advertising approach.*

"That will be the account executive's responsibility, too. Whether he brings the thinking out of the group or develops it himself, he's the man who must stimulate the thinking."

5. *Learn how to write an ad, a letter, a publicity release, a sales presentation, a radio or TV announcement.*

"Unless you learn how to do those things, you are not in a position to judge too well the work of other people."

6. *Work efficiently with other departments, keeping them fully informed.*

"We've had instances where departments have wasted a tremendous amount of time running down some blind alley, doing the job wrong, because the account executive had never taken the time to tell them how the job was supposed to be done."

7. *Learn how to sell the client's product to the consumer.*

"Every account executive must go out and sell his client's product with the client's salesmen so that he knows the problems of the sales force firsthand."

8. *Keep a scrapbook of ideas.*

"There are few new ideas. There are few people in the world who create really new thoughts. The creative people I know are men who wrestle with problems and read and study what other people are doing and adapt thoughts of others and twist them around to where they can use them to their own advantage. You can't begin to realize your potential without keeping a file of ideas."

9. *Learn to diagnose potential trouble spots months before trouble occurs.*

"Always be on the alert for trouble. Don't wait until the client raises hell about something, but anticipate. Develop a personal butt-kicking philosophy. It's a lot better to kick your own self in the behind than it is to wait until somebody else does it. It's a lot less painful when you do it yourself."

10. *Learn to think.*

"It doesn't take a creative genius to develop sales and advertising ideas. It's simply a matter of learning to work at it."

11. *Read the trade papers.*

"The trade papers give you a feeling for the business. They enable you to talk to your client in his own terminology. They keep you abreast of what's going on."

12. *Cover all client calls with a conference report.*

"Every call where a decision is made calling for help from one of the departments or committing the agency for money must be covered in a conference report. This prevents misunderstandings between you and the client."

With that, Morris passed out the Self-Analysis Questionnaire, the crescendo of the morning's meeting. He wanted his account executives to hold up a mirror to their performance and take a critical look. The form included 19 questions, many of them of the yes-or-no variety. It measured an ad person's performance inside-out.

Hite had set out a work ethic he expected his staff to emulate. He wanted them to dedicate themselves to advertising 24 hours a day, seven days a week and 52 weeks a year. That's all.

CHAPTER THREE

"NOW THAT YOU'RE AN ACCOUNT EXECUTIVE, YOU'LL FIND OUT HOW TOUGH IT IS TO GET THOSE CREATIVE GUYS TO WRITE IT AND DRAW IT THE WAY YOU *KNOW* IT OUGHT TO BE DONE."—MORRIS HITE

Over the first three months of 1957, Tracy-Locke's account service staff listened to 12 Monday morning sermons of the advertising gospel according to Morris Hite.

He began the meetings precisely at 7 a.m. and held forth for two hours. He based his remarks partly on his own experiences, partly on his extensive reading about advertising and partly on his intuition about how businessmen think and how the business world works.

Hite spiced his lectures with a salty tongue. In announcing the training program, Hite had written in a memorandum, "If any women elect to attend, they must do so with the understanding that they will have to listen to some foul language. I will conduct the sessions and must have complete freedom of expression."

Hite had complete freedom of expression—and freedom in everything else. He was free to make the rules and free to change them.

Tracy-Locke's account service people were free, too. They were free not to be late to any of the sessions, free not to miss any of the sessions without a catastrophic excuse and free not to forget to bring with them the homework project Hite had assigned at the end of the previous session.

The homework assignments ranged from developing

a marketing plan to creating an ad campaign to writing sample headlines for sample ads. Taking a page from Izaak Walton, Morris was angling to create the Compleat Account Executive.

Hite believed that the best adman was a generalist, not a specialist, someone with interdisciplinary skills. He recognized that within the overall umbrella of advertising an adman would have stronger and weaker ribs. But he also knew that if an adman had a basic competence in each of the specific advertising disciplines, from sales promotion to direct mail, he could create more selling opportunities for clients.

Hite didn't care which communications techniques were employed, so long as they achieved sales increases for his clients. Such measures of advertising effectiveness as brand awareness, advertising recall and corporate image made less of an impression on Morris than sales.

Sales increases for clients ranked as job one at Tracy-Locke. As Morris might have put it: *If a client's cash registers aren't ringing, what the hell good is a positive product image?*

Session Two: MARKETING PLANS

Morris Hite stressed that a client's marketing plan represents the blueprint for an ad agency's client service. A marketing plan specifies sales objectives, provides a rationale for those objectives and suggests the steps by which they will be met. Since the agency account executive must implement the marketing plan, it stands to reason he or she should be responsible for creating it.

Hite told his account service people collectively what he often told them individually: "The ultimate test of a finished account executive is his ability to write a sound marketing plan."

According to Hite, a marketing plan consisted of six steps, which moved sequentially and logically:

Step One: *Analyze the situation and set up goals and objectives.*

"That means collecting all pertinent data—like sales figures broken down by specific sales territories. It means analyzing competitive brand positions, by consumer studies or by contact with the client's sales force or through personal observations in stores. You must also be able to use primary and secondary research, whether collected by Tracy-Locke's field staff or from newspapers and other media."

Step Two: *Get full of your subject.*

"Assemble all the pertinent information you can. Use books by experts on the subject or government bulletins from the Department of Commerce or Department of Agriculture, or from trade magazines. And it's not enough to just have information about your own client. You have to know about your competitors' programs, their advertising and merchandising and packaging. And you damn well better know their pricing structure and the quality of their product."

Step Three: *Hunt for the Big Idea.*

"Use your heads. Think. Study what other folks have done in competitive and non-competitive lines. We keep files and scrapbooks around here, use them. Talk to consumers and dealers about the product. Find out what the motivation research says about consumers' attitudes toward the product. All the information you need to do your job well is out there waiting for you to grab hold of it."

Step Four: *Write an outline.*

"Forcing yourself to commit your thinking to paper will help you refine it and shape it. That's true, gentlemen, whether you're writing a speech or any kind of presentation. You have to know where you're going before you can get there."

Step Five: *Collect All Materials.*

"You have to coordinate all the elements you'll need to present the finished marketing plan with other departments. Give the art department what it needs to create any ads or point-of-sale art you may need. Give data to the media department for the media analysis. Get everyone involved who needs to be involved."

Step Six: *Write the plan.*

"A lot of you probably think a marketing plan is nothing but a pain in the ass. You're probably asking yourself why should you even bother to write the goddamn thing. Well, I'll tell you why. The marketing plan forces account executives to *think* and from that thinking comes *ideas,* and those ideas are what help the accounts grow. And as a result, this agency grows, too. Do I make myself clear?"

"The marketing plan also provides a blueprint for the account executive to follow throughout the year," Morris continued. "That eliminates a lot of wasted time and motion and it eliminates your constantly having to fight against deadlines. The plan provides information and guidance for department heads. And one other thing: It gives us the opportunity to resell the client each year. It gives us a chance to show them how we've helped them build their business. We don't have to blow smoke about our performance, we have a document to use to sit down and show them exactly what we've done. It's like money in the bank."

Hite wrapped up the session by making a homework assignment: Everyone had until April 1 to write a complete marketing plan for one of Tracy-Locke's clients. And they had until the following Monday to write a report on what they considered to be the best advertising and merchandising plan they had observed in 1956.

Session Three: SUCCESSFUL ACCOUNT EXECUTIVES

As Morris Hite presented his "Ten Qualities A Man Must Have To Be A Successful Account Executive," he pointed out that the term 'account executive' should be synonymous with 'consumer marketing executive.' Hite's ideal account man didn't restrict his role to the confines of advertising; he did everything in his power to help sell the product: sales, marketing, promotion, publicity—you name it.

HITE'S TEN QUALITIES FOR SUCCESS:

1. *Must Be a Well-Rounded Businessman.*

"You have to understand sales at all levels, and you must read business publications like *Time, Fortune* and *The Wall Street Journal* so you can speak to sales managers on their own level."

2. *Must Have Leadership.*

"You're the quarterback of the agency team. You must sell all the agency departments on doing their best job."

3. *Must Have An Inquisitive Mind.*

"You've got to be sales-wise. During your leisure moments you must be thinking about your clients' problems."

4. *Must Have Thinking Capacity.*

"The art of thinking is hard work, and the good account executive has an appetite for it. Don't settle for the first thought that comes to mind, because everybody else has thought of that."

5. *Must Have Detail Capacity.*

"If the budget is likely to be overspent, you have to figure out the reason why before it happens and prevent it.

You have to be detail-oriented enough to make sure that a 10-second commercial gets to station WHAT at 9:51 on a Tuesday morning. There's a lot of day-in and day-out drudgery to the business, but an account executive takes responsibility for every action. He can't tell himself, or anyone else, 'I'm pretty smart myself—I just have some pretty stupid people helping me.' He's responsible for all of it."

6. *Must Have A Love of People.*

"This one's self-explanatory. Advertising is a people business. Always has been, always will be."

7. *Must Handle People With Tact and Self-Confidence.*

"An account executive must be able to get along with people, and when I say that, I mean all people. It helps if you learn people's names and call them by their names. It's also nice to know little things about them, like their families and hobbies. Take an active interest in other people and you will command their respect."

8. *Must Be Mentally Flexible.*

"I like to see account executives who stand firm when their position is borne out by facts. At the same time, you need to be open-minded to the opinions of others. And no account executive should ever be afraid to admit a mistake. We all make them. I've never met anyone yet who didn't."

9. *Must Love His Work.*

"The demands on account executives are greater than in any other area of advertising. You have the overall responsibility."

10. *Must Have A Deep Sense of Loyalty.*

"You have allegiance both to the agency and your clients. In reality, you have two bosses. Me and the client."

Hite closed session three by reading aloud an article called "What An Advertiser Wants From Account Management." The article, written by a General Foods marketing executive, said that advertisers expected agencies to be partners not hucksters, executives not geniuses. Clients expected agencies to operate with calm judgment and dignity, not operate as a messenger service. Hite had come across the article in a trade magazine. While *idea-hunting*.

Session Four: SELLING STRATEGIES

In week four, Hite focused his attention on creating basic selling strategies for advertising programs. "Remember," he told the group, "Nobody is interested in a product *per se*. People are interested in what products will do for them."

Morris explained that consumers buy products based on perceived benefits. The benefits might be to satisfy basic needs for safety or security. They might satisfy requirements for transportation. Or even an individual's requirements for power, prestige or status.

Drawing on successful case histories from Tracy-Locke and other ad agencies, Morris spent the next two hours working his way through a checklist of 11 basic appeals that can be used to formulate advertising strategies:

1. Will the product make the purchaser feel more important? How?
2. Will the product make the purchaser happier? Why?
3. Will the product make the purchaser more comfortable? When?
4. Will the product make the purchaser more prosperous? How?
5. Will the product make work easier for the purchaser? How much easier?
6. Will the product give the purchaser more security? How?

7. Will the product make the purchaser more attractive or better liked? How?

8. Will the product give the purchaser some distinction? In what way?

9. Will the product improve, protect or maintain the purchaser's health? How?

10. Will the product appeal to the purchaser as a bargain? Why?

11. Will the product offer the purchaser more value or service than competitive products.

Morris emphasized that advertising messages have strategic functions. Ad messages isolate opportunities for a client to sell his product by pushing hot buttons to consumer response. Ad messages aren't happenstance, willy-nilly creations that result from a quick-witted individual dreaming up something clever to say. Ad messages stem from strategic objectives, plotted out in an orderly, methodical fashion. The good ones, anyway.

Session Five: CREATING AN AD

Morris began the "How to Write An Ad" session by telling the story of an adman who said "Whenever I have to write a headline [for an ad], I imagine that some disinterested person is just leaving my office. As he gets to the door, I must say something about the product or its benefits that will make him stop, turn around, come back into my office and ask me to tell him more about it."

"The headline is the most important element of an ad," said Hite. "It must offer a promise to the reader of a believable benefit. And it must be phrased in a way to give it memory value." He cited devices like alliteration, comparisons, balanced phrases and rhyming as devices for adding memory value.

Hite compared direct headlines, which are informative and get immediately to the point, with indirect headlines, which do not. The advantage of direct headlines, or hard-sell headlines, is that they convey the basic sales message at a quick glance. The disadvantage is that they give readers little incentive to read further.

Indirect headlines, by contrast, provide incentive to read further, but run the risk of failing to engage the reader from the outset. "An agency that uses indirect headlines bets the advertiser's dollars on its ability to make people read the body text," he said. "If that fails, the advertisement has less value than one with a direct headline . . . sometimes no value at all."

Hite, who preferred a strong selling message in headlines, suggested that most effective ads often have a combination headline that includes a selling proposition with a hint of a more expansive theme.

"A little curiosity and a touch of imagination lifts advertising out of the rut," he said, citing as an example Tracy-Locke's own work for Maryland Club coffee. There's no comparison between:

"The coffee you'd drink if you were a millionaire,"

and

"The coffee you'd drink if you owned all the coffee in the world."

Session Six: PERSUASIVE WRITING

Having given his staff their headlines, Morris moved on to the broader issue of persuasive writing—ad copy, business letters, memoranda, conference reports. He cast an immediate recommendation for the KISS (Keep It Simple, Stupid) school of wordsmanship.

"You must write so anyone can understand what you're saying," said Hite. "Even smart people have to divide their energies between making out what the words are all about and sizing up the proposition. Don't let the words get in their own way."

Morris himself never used a ten-cent word when a

five-cent word would do. He used short words, short sentences and short paragraphs. Always.

He recommended that Tracy-Locke account executives read books like "How To Write Advertising Copy" by Ken Goode and "The Art of Readable Writing" by Rudolf Flesch and "My Life in Advertising" by Claude Hopkins to hone their writing talents.

Turning to the subject of ad copy, Morris stressed the need for copy to flow in a logical, proper sequence. "Readers should not be urged to buy until he's been given reasons why he should want the product," he said.

Be specific.

"General information is not persuasive. For a TV advertiser to say his set produces a picture that is 'clear, sharp and excitingly real,' is merely a general claim true of any good TV set. But to say 'clear, sharp pictures on the only tube guaranteed for three years,' gives information exclusive to that particular set."

Avoid abstract adjectives.

"After you finish your copy go back and cut out most of the adjectives. And be careful not to use abstract words, because they are lazy words. Be descriptive and be selective in your choice of words."

Session Seven: MERCHANDISING

By the halfway point of the Account Executive's Training School, Morris' mood had brightened considerably. He could sense that his account executives had new enthusiasm for their daily assignments. And the bitching and moaning about the Monday morning sessions had eased.

Hite felt chipper enough to turn the session on merchandising over to one of Tracy-Locke's account men, Bill James. James had been working for the California Cling

Peach Advisory Board in 1948 when he called on Borden's Dallas plant manager to solicit participation in an in-store promotion for peaches and cottage cheese. The Borden people referred James to Morris Hite at Tracy-Locke and made it clear that if Hite liked James' idea, so would they.

As it turned out Hite liked both James and his idea. A few years later, James joined the Tracy-Locke payroll. Before turning over the floor to James, Hite drew a critical distinction: "Advertising moves people toward goods; merchandising moves goods toward people."

James shared a few case histories from Tracy-Locke's past, recapping how the agency had been involved with merchandising events like cookbook promotions for Imperial Sugar, tavern taste-tests for Regal Beer and recipe books for Fritos corn chips. "To see merchandising opportunities you have to know the client's business and be completely familiar with his *sales* problems," chimed in Hite.

Session Eight: MARKETING RESEARCH

In session eight, Hite shared the platform with his crack researchers, Bud Phillips and Jack Taylor. Though few ad agencies outside of New York and Chicago delved into marketing research in 1957, Tracy-Locke had been a pioneer in the Southwest.

"Research should be used to stimulate thinking and to add to thinking," insisted Morris, who considered marketing a three-sided proposition. "By that I mean clients have a view of their business, the ad agency has a separate view and the consumer a third view. But the most important thing for any business is to know how its customer thinks and to understand its customer's problems."

Phillips and Taylor outlined for the account executives the range of Tracy-Locke's research activities: marketing research, consumer research and depth motivational research. The agency's main tool was consumer research, compiled through responses to structured questionnaires given to scientifically drawn samples of people. The agency had increased its use of depth motivational research, using small samples of "focus groups" in unstructured conversations.

"The thing I want to stress is that continuous research can often save manufacturers and advertising agencies from suffering sales decreases because they point out problems well in advance," said Hite.

Session Nine: DIRECT MAIL

Morris' pet subjects included direct mail advertising, a genre in which he'd worked early in his advertising career.

"The key to a successful direct mail effort is the sales letter," he said. "The first paragraph serves the same function as the headline in an ad. You must get the reader's attention and you must promise him a benefit." Six strong words to key the first paragraph were:

New
Easy
You
How
These
Which . . .?

Hite discussed techniques for improving the response rates, like personalizing the letter and inserting reply cards. "When you think about it, all advertising is geared to buying customers," said Morris. "The direct mail person knows what conversion ratio is necessary to ensure his profitable operation."

Session Ten: TV COMMERCIALS

Although by 1957 Tracy-Locke had scored some noticeable success with TV campaigns, notably for Imperial Sugar and Haggar Apparel, print advertising remained the agency's dominant medium for revenue. That would change within a few short years, however, as television penetrated a greater number of American households and, with the refinement of color, became the dominant media. Not only for entertainment, but for news and information.

Hite weighed the critical issues of the time:

Live TV versus Film.

"Live commercials have the appeal of immediacy. Film controls the quality of message."

Network versus spot market buys.

"Network programs offer prestige and greater memorability. Spot offers greater frequency and affordability."

Length of TV spots.

"Sixty-second work well for new products; 20-second spots give you more availabilities to select from."

Television commercials, said Hite, should perform five functions:

1. Be Built Around a Powerful Selling Idea
2. Have Immediate Impact
3. Have Incessant Interest
4. Convey Information
5. Give Viewers A Strong Impulse to Buy

"Make sure you've got 'attention bait' before you hit viewers with the pitch," said Hite. "If you don't have their interest at the beginning, they won't be around when you get to the sell.

"And one more thing," he added. "Don't fall into the trap of designing what you believe the client will buy, as opposed to what you sincerely believe is good advertising."

Session Eleven: SALES PROMOTION

Hite explained that sales promotions typically involve consumer incentives (such as a cents-off coupon discount, or buy one, get a second one half-price) and usually require action within a specified time limit.

Sales Promotions are often used to introduce new products, change buy habits, force distribution, to fight back competition, to influence dealers or salesmen. They often take the form of Sampling offers, Premium offers, Contests or Price Deals. Properly planned and executed, they can have significant short-term impact.

Session Twelve: IT'S A WRAP

Hite conducted the final training session on April 1, advancing the idea that account executives can be characterized as either craftsmen or marketers.

Craftsmen react to their clients' needs. Craftsman can create TV commercials or print campaigns, magazine ads pretty as you please, but they take their cues from the client. Marketers take charge. Marketers are methodical in their approach, motivated by potential sales increases. Marketers don't follow clients, they lead them.

Morris Hite, marketer, intended to mold Tracy-Locke's account men into marketers, too.

CHAPTER FOUR

"GIVE ME A NUMBER TWO PENCIL AND A BIG CHIEF TABLET AND I'LL WRITE IT MYSELF."—MORRIS HITE

How did Morris Hite know enough about advertising to conduct his own 12-week training course in the beginning of 1957?

Simple—experience.

Then 46, Hite had worked in the advertising business for 30 years. Beginning at 16, he handled publicity and promotion, worked as a mechanical artist doing ad layouts and wrote promotional copy. In his 20s, he ran his own small agency in Oklahoma City, doing all the things a one-man operator must do to survive.

By the time he hooked up with Tracy-Locke-Dawson in Dallas in 1937, Morris had tried his hand at virtually every phase of persuasive communications and demonstrated at least a journeyman's ability in each of them. He could write a little and draw a little—and he could sell a lot.

Advertising obsessed Morris Hite. Had businessmen in the 1940s and 1950s been called "workaholics," he would have qualified. Hite put in long hours at Tracy-Locke, kept sketch pads at his home to rough out ideas in the evenings and traveled extensively on client business. "Sometimes I think the airlines and the telephone company make more money out of our business than we do," he observed.

He generally worked a seven-day week. Always on Saturday and usually on Sunday. "What do you mean you've got more than you can do?" he'd say to anyone who complained about the workload. "I haven't seen you around the office on Saturday or Sunday lately."

Hite loved the fact that every day's a new day in sales and marketing. Situations constantly change, presenting business executives with new sets of problems. Only in Morris's view, clients didn't have problems, they had *opportunities*. He put a positive spin on situations, and his attitude could be contagious with clients and colleagues.

Lewis Torrance, who became president of the Borden Inc. dairy division in the 1970s, first met Morris Hite in 1937. Hite, then a young account executive with Tracy-Locke-Dawson, helped Borden with the publicity and promotion in Oklahoma City following its acquisition of Evans Milk Co. Hite knew the right people in the state capital to ensure that Borden received a proper welcome from city fathers.

Torrance recalls the energy and enthusiasm of the young account man. "Morris was a slender fellow, skinny almost, and what you might call 'hyper.' He could hardly sit still. He walked fast and talked fast and whenever an idea came up he would say 'Let's go do it. Let's take care of business.'

"Morris had a charisma about him," said Torrance. "He was a two-fisted guy, he'd done some boxing and some fight promoting you know, and there wasn't any problem he wouldn't tackle. It didn't have to be just in marketing or advertising, either. Before he'd leave your office he'd help you solve *all* your problems."

Borden officials considered Hite to be more than an adman. "As the years went on, we came to regard Morris as a sales manager in his own right. We never had a sales meeting without him. We'd bring him in on our operations meetings, too. He knew that much about the milk and ice cream business."

Hite learned Borden's business the way he learned the business of all his ad accounts: from the ground up. Assigned to the Borden account, Hite began rising before dawn and making deliveries with the Borden route men. He conducted a fact-finding mission of his own.

Morris loaded the milk truck, making sure the product was iced down properly. He accompanied the route man into the local grocery store, checking the dairy case to see how much milk had been sold, if any had been damaged, how much needed to be restocked. He took time to study the grocer's dairy case, checking the pricing and packaging of competitive products. He chatted with the grocer to get the merchant's point of view.

And when Hite saw a shopper taking milk from the dairy case, he'd introduce himself: *"Excuse me, why are you buying this particular milk? Is it because of freshness? Taste? The carton? The price? Something else?"*

Before Morris would presume to know enough about a product or service to advertise it, he felt he had to understand that total sales environment. Not just for Borden's milk, but for Mrs Baird's Bread and Imperial Sugar and the other accounts he handled. How were their products manufactured and distributed? How were they sold? What were the critical junctures from production to end-use?

Hite had the perfect tools for such fact-finding: an inquisitive mind and an appetite for discovery. He also believed an advertising account man belonged out in the sales arena, not seated behind a desk. The adman needed to be in the field, talking to salesmen and customers alike, listening and learning. (Forty years after Hite began working on Borden, Tracy-Locke account executives still received on-the-job training by accompanying the delivery man on his rounds.)

Hite had been self-educated. He never finished high school, hardly got started in fact. Morris once told a copywriter being hired at Tracy-Locke, "Don't be so smug you only have a high school education. I only finished the 10th grade." Even so, his maternal grandparents, who raised Morris after his father deserted the family and his mother died young, instilled in their grandson the value of an education. If not a formal one, then catch-as-catch can.

Hite caught their drift. From his pre-teenage days, when he wrote off for a correspondence course to learn cartoon illustration, Morris never stopped reading, talking, thinking, learning: acquiring knowledge he could put to use on behalf of his ad clients; gaining a Solomon-like wisdom that would bring businessmen from other fields to his door seeking counsel; developing a perspective that in his later years would enable him to play a role in the economic expansion of the Dallas/Fort Worth area.

Even as the world grew increasingly complex during his lifetime, Hite retained an ability to cut to the heart of a business problem. He could strip back the layers of tertiary issues and concentrate on the core. He also possessed a sixth sense about how one decision would influence a subsequent chain of events. To native intuition he added a thought process conditioned by years of idea-hunting. The result: an adman who knew business, talked business, and didn't have to b.s. his way through life.

Morris passed on to his captive audience at the Tracy-Locke training school the essence of his own experience, a distillation of successful marketing techniques he had seen, done or heard about.

Take product positioning. Hite shared the story of how Tracy-Locke had helped position Dr Pepper as a source of energy as well as refreshment. The agency's durable ad slogan, "Drink a Bite to Eat at 10, 2 and 4 O'Clock" promoted the idea that a non-cola soft drink could counteract the energy lags that people experience during the day. The idea helped Dr Pepper, a fruit-flavored carbonated drink that enjoys a loyal brand following, gain a spate of national attention and significant market share.

Take product claims. Hite himself conceived the idea of selling Borden's buttermilk as a curative for holiday season hangovers. He created an ad campaign especially for the last two weeks of December and the first week of January based on the idea: "Bounce Back With Buttermilk." As a merchandising tie-in, Hite created a "sympathy" card so that friends could send their friends a 20-quart jug of buttermilk accompanied with the "Sorry About Your Hangover."

Take product benefits. For Maryland Club Coffee, Hite and Tracy-Locke created a campaign promising consumers a touch of class. In a category considered to be price sensitive, shoppers suddenly had a new reason, prestige, to pay several cents more per pound. Hite took the same approach with Borden's "Lady Borden" ice cream. His slogan, "Fit for a golden spoon," set the brand apart from other pedestrian ice creams, which presumably were fit only for silver spoons.

For Imperial Sugar, Morris centered the product benefit on helping Helen Housewife in the proving ground of the '40s and '50s, the kitchen. Tracy-Locke's selling strategy conveyed the message *Be the best cook in your crowd*. Helen Housewife could accomplish that by using Imperial Sugar's cookbooks and brochures, available for a nominal price by mailing in the Pure Sugar Cane label from a specified number of bags. The literature, written by a number of Tracy-Locke wordsmiths, Hite included, revealed helpful hints like "How To Have A Meet-Your-Neighbor Party." The gist seemed to be 'serve them sweets baked with Imperial Sugar.'

To cultivate Helen Housewife's daughters and nieces as future Imperial Sugar consumers, Hite created a teen-aged spokescharacter named Teena, who had some recipes of her own to share with the future homemakers of Texas. Imperial received more than 500,000 requests for "Teena's Cookbook," which would have made the best-seller lists.

For Haggar Co., Hite created a "Harmony Chart" that enabled customers to work with color combinations of jackets and pants. Tracy-Locke promoted the idea of extending a wardrobe by mixing two pairs of Haggar slacks with a sport coat. Hite had come up with the idea while *idea-hunting*: He'd seen a paint company's chart of paints to match for house and trim.

For Mrs Baird's Bakeries, Hite geared the selling effort to freshness and family. A biographical ad campaign depicted the Fort Worth family's enterprise begun by Mrs. Ninnie L. Baird after the death of her husband and carried on by several generations of Bairds. "Stays fresh longer" read the advertising, "From the Baird family to you."

Morris Hite hoped to impart to his account men more than proven ad techniques, however. He wanted them to share his sense of urgency. He'd overcome humble origins and made himself into a successful businessman. As one of his Tracy-Locke employees once observed: "Morris made a million dollars in advertising. If he'd have been in any other business, he'd have made $10 million."

Hite succeeded by being ambitious, strong-willed and totally committed to his clients' business. He hoped that long after his account men had forgotten about his training lectures they would still remember his personal creed:

There's no substitute for total commitment.

CHAPTER FIVE

"A PAT ON THE FANNY GETS YOU FURTHER THAN A KICK IN THE BUTT."—MORRIS HITE

Morris Lee Hite, Jr. was born on November 23, 1910, in Anadarko, Oklahoma, three years and a week after Oklahoma gained statehood. He became the first and only child born to Morris Lee Hite and Marie Campbell Hite.

Hite's father, called Lee, and his father's two younger brothers, Boone and Ormsby Hite, enjoyed their status as prominent businessmen in the bustling town of Anadarko. They owned the Anadarko State Bank and operated a prosperous farm on the edge of town.

In truth, Lee preferred ranching and working cattle to any other gainful enterprise. So did Ormsby. They let brother Boone handle most of the family's business.

Boone Hite liked to wheel-and-deal. He won the deed of ownership to an Indian trading post near Anadarko in a game of draw poker. He used the trading post to set up a loan business, lending some of his excess cash to Indians from the nearby Kiowa reservation. He charged the Indians exorbitant interest rates and used the profits to help bankroll his other investments, which included banking and real estate.

A dreamer, schemer and natural-born promoter, Boone Hite envisioned major development around Anadarko. Anadarko had been built in 1901, on Indian Territory the U.S. government had acquired from the Kiowa nation. It's located in the central part of Oklahoma, roughly 45 miles southwest of Oklahoma City.

In 1910, Boone Hite produced a sales brochure aimed

at attracting new business to the area. He proclaimed Anadarko as the "Pearl of the Washita," a reference to the Washita River that flowed through the center of town. The brochure featured photographs of the downtown business area, the cotton mill, church, school, court house and city hall, as well as several pictures labeled the "Hite Bros. Farm."

Among their business interests, the Hite brothers owned and operated several small banks. To ensure that Caddo County funds would be deposited in their Anadarko State Bank, the outspoken Boone had talked his tight-lipped brother Lee into running for County Treasurer. Boone steered his older brother's campaign, of course.

Lee Hite, a reticent man, cringed at the idea of making a speech in public. Nevertheless, on the eve of the election he mounted the platform at the town meeting and said his piece: "I'm Lee Hite. I'm running for County Treasurer. Look me over. If I look all right to you, I'd appreciate your vote. Now I'm going down the street to the Red Horse Saloon and I'll buy everybody a drink who wants to come with me." He won by a landslide.

What would likely have been a well-to-do upbringing for Morris Lee Hite Jr. began unraveling even before he grew out of diapers. A series of financial misfortunes befell the Hite brothers. First Ormsby overextended himself trying to establish a horse-and-mule business. Then an outbreak of cholera ravaged the Hite brothers' hog farming operations, claiming more than a 1,000 head.

The Hite brothers didn't have a monopoly on bad luck. A drought hit central Oklahoma in the early 1910s, taking the cash out of cash crops like wheat and hay. Farmers and ranchers scarcely had enough money to feed their families, much less to repay their loans to the Hite-owned banks.

The brothers watched their bad debt rise month after month, until insolvency seemed inevitable. Then Boone, ever the gambler, devised a plan to try to save the Hite brothers' fortune. He convinced Lee and Ormsby to agree to pool their remaining assets and put them into a wildcat drilling program.

With the Hite's financial empire on the brink, Boone promptly went out and drilled seven oil wells. He hit seven dry holes. Dusters.

Financially ruined, the Hites dissolved their partnership. Boone and Lee left Anadarko for Oklahoma City, while Ormsby moved to western Oklahoma and found work on a ranch. Lee landed a job with the State of Oklahoma, overseeing a controversial disease-control program for cattle. The state program aroused such bitter controversy that he packed a pistol at all times and slept with his gun under his pillow. He traveled alone, which he seemed to prefer.

Lee left behind his young wife Marie and Morris Lee Jr. to endure a hardscrabble existence of their own. They lived with her parents, George and Mahaly Campbell, but health complications that followed her giving birth to her son forced Marie in and out of hospitals. She never fully recovered from a bout with tuberculosis, and died just as young Morris reached school age.

Despite the devastation of being left without parents, Morris Hite grew up a good-natured, happy child. Morris, who adopted the name his father shunned, made good marks in school, enjoyed baseball, track and other sports, and took part in the Boy Scouts of America program. He came to admire his grandparents for their honesty, integrity and self-sufficiency. He tried to copy their humility.

Morris soon discovered that he possessed an ability to draw. He made free-hand pencil sketches of animals, windmills, landscapes, things he saw around his hometown. He sent off for a correspondence course in cartooning to further his talent and, with a neighborhood friend named Ross Hume, he collaborated on the unofficial sequel to *Gulliver's*

Travels. The *Oklahoma Times* ran a story about the young artist.

Morris' grandfather impressed on the young boy the value of reading. In the evenings, while other folks in Anadarko sat on their front porches and gossiped, the Campbell clan gathered in their living room. Grandfather Campbell read aloud to his grandson, an experience that influenced Morris' lifelong interest in books and literature.

Other than his special interests in drawing and reading, young Morris Hite lived the life of a typical country boy growing up in Oklahoma in the 1920s. He awoke early to do his daily chores, which included milking the cow. He ate a hearty breakfast, then headed out for school. After school he'd do more chores at his grandparents' bidding, or play with his neighborhood friends. Occasionally, he'd slip off and fish in the Washita River.

But even at an early age, Morris Hite showed a knack for salesmanship. As he said in a 1979 interview with *Dallas* magazine:

"My grandparents weren't poor people, but they weren't well off, either. They taught me how to work. We had dewberries and plums, and I would pick them and sell them house to house because you could get a better price that way than you could selling to the grocery stores. I milked a cow and sold all the milk that the three of us didn't use. I had a few customers that I delivered to every day after milking."

Milking a Jersey cow each morning helped Morris form more than the callouses on the his hands. The experience helped him form an outlook on life. A half century later, in many of his frequent public appearances, Morris said he learned four important lessons from that Jersey cow.

Lesson one came from being swatted in the face time after time by the cow's cockleburred tail. "I learned forbearance, understanding and forgiveness. I also learned to concentrate on the job at hand and not to be distracted by moments of discomfort."

Lesson two dealt with encouragement. Hite discovered that the cow, like all of God's creatures, responded to positive reinforcement. In other words, "A pat on the fanny gets you further than a kick in the butt."

Lesson three came from the output of the cow, which taught Hite how persistence pays off. "You learn from milking that the last strippings yield the richest cream."

Lesson four came with Morris' realization that if he treated the cow as she wanted to be treated, keeping her contented, she'd produce more milk. And more milk meant more money for Morris. "I learned that the customer always comes first. You have to keep him happy before you do anything else."

The lessons Morris learned milking the Jersey cow helped prepare him for his career in advertising. Nothing, however, could have prepared him for the next chapter of his life.

CHAPTER SIX

"I HAD A WAY OF ATTRACTING NUTS."—MORRIS HITE

Gulliver's Travels, the inspiration for some of Hite's early artwork, seemed no more curious than Morris's own travels. In the fall of 1926, Morris accepted an invitation to take part in a work-study program through Arnett Athenaeum.

Located near Oklahoma City and ostensibly an institute of higher learning, Arnett engaged in the eclectic pursuits of an eccentric man named Eugene Arnett. Arnett recruited male students, typically high school seniors or freshmen from the nearby University of Oklahoma, to assist with a mail-order operation he housed at the Athenaeum. The students, who worked half a day in exchange for tuition fees, ran the printing presses, filled the mail orders, swept the floors and kept the operation running.

In the spring of 1926, Arnett, looking for a cartoonist to help illustrate his sales literature, had asked A.C. Streeter, principal of Anadarko High, to recommend any young artists he might know. Streeter had just the person in mind: Morris Hite. A good student and hard worker, no troublemaker at all, Hite possessed such maturity beyond his 15 years that Arnett made an exception to his policy of hiring older boys. He offered Morris room and board and a small weekly salary. He promised to arrange for Hite to attend classes at Putnam H.S. near the Athenaeum.

By then, Morris believed he'd become a burden to his aging grandparents. He wanted to be closer to Lee Hite and Uncle Boone, who were both living in Oklahoma City. Mostly, Morris wanted to be on his own.

He moved into Arnett Athenaeum in the fall of 1926.

Upon his arrival, Hite asked the caretaker, "What business are we in?"

"I don't know. You'll have to ask the gardener," came the caretaker's reply. "I've only been here four years."

Morris learned from his fellow workers that his new boss had made his money selling life insurance. The story went that Mr. Arnett had sold so much life insurance that his individual commissions put one company in financial jeopardy, and the company subsequently offered him a large cash settlement as severance pay. Arnett had used some of the money to buy the building in which he set up the Athenaeum, then started direct selling. When Morris arrived, the main product was men's work shoes, which were stacked all around the building.

To his chagrin and dismay, Hite discovered shortly that Arnett's principal pursuit involved rewriting the Bible. Arnett told Morris that future generations of mankind would abandon the scriptures in favor of *Biological Christianity* by Eugene Arnett.

Arnett, obviously, had been a half-century ahead of his time. In the late 1970s, he might have been a TV evangelist. Instead, he spent most of his waking hours sitting stark naked in a brass cupola atop his building typing away on his revisions to the Old and New Testaments.

Hite wrestled with heading back to Anadarko High, but ultimately chose to put up with Arnett's kookiness. "I felt disgusted, as if I'd been robbed," he said. "I thought I was in a nut house. But Arnett was a very articulate guy, very intense, with almost hypnotic eyes. He needed a lot of flunkies around the place to run the printing presses, get the mail and do all kinds of odd jobs. One guy had the job of making up great quantities of cultured buttermilk, which Arnett drank for some kind of stomach problem. He was convinced that was the only way he could stay alive."

Hite's decision to stay on at the Athenaeum introduced him to his life's work. "In the evenings, after my chores and homework were done and there was nothing left to do, I'd spend a lot of time in Arnett's library. That's one thing I'll always be grateful to the old man for, he was constantly lecturing us on the need to read, to learn, to be informed."

Hite came across bound volumes of a magazine called *Printer's Ink*, dating back to the first issue in 1895. The magazine covered the advertising and print production trades, areas in which Arnett needed expertise to run his mail-order business. "I began reading those things and I became fascinated with advertising. I decided it was a business I'd like to try."

Each night, Hite spent hours reading about ad agencies in New York and Chicago, those faraway places, and about the people who created the ads he saw in *Collier's, Look, Saturday Evening Post* and other magazines. Morris began to recognize the art of persuasion. He studied not only the words and the images of advertisements, but the selling strategy being used.

After a year with Arnett, 16-year-old Morris Hite wished to be reacquainted with the real world. He headed to Oklahoma City, where he signed on as a trainee in the advertising department of the *Oklahoma City News*.

Morris' newspaper career proved to be no longer than a coffee break. While *Printer's Ink* had taught Morris a great deal about advertising, or so he thought, it had failed to teach him that newspaper ads are measured in column inches, not square inches.

The first time Hite ordered cuts for a department store ad, he gave the measurement in square inches. The cuts didn't fit, botching the insertion. The advertiser raised a stink. Hite got fired on the spot.

"I didn't know what a column inch was," he admitted, "but I learned an invaluable lesson that day." From then on, Morris made it his business to find out every detail of an assignment.

Hite's first crack at advertising had been inauspicious, but he soon showed his innate marketing savvy. He landed a job in 1927 with Griffith Amusement Co., operators of movie houses in the Oklahoma towns of Norman and Ardmore. With the advent of talking pictures—Al Jolson made "The Jazz Singer" that same year—Americans had started going to movies in record numbers.

Hite's job, for which he was paid $20 a week, involved working three days a week in Norman and three in Ardmore, and traveling by bus between the two towns on his day off. Morris sold tickets, passed out handbills, collected merchandise to be given away at "country store night" and did anything he could to build traffic at the box office.

Morris' most inspired idea came before the premiere in Ardmore of a Wallace Beery comedy about aviation called "Now We Are In The Air." Hite knew about a private plane that had been in a crash sitting inoperable at the local air strip. In the middle of the night, he towed the airplane to downtown Ardmore and set up a mock crash that made it look as if a plane had crashed into the movie theater.

The next morning, the town of Ardmore buzzed about Hite's publicity stunt. And the next evening, moviegoers filled every seat in the house.

Despite such a flair for the dramatic, Morris couldn't see his movie career headed for Hollywood. After one too many bumpy bus rides between Norman and Ardmore, he decided to move on. He hitchhiked back to Oklahoma City and found a job at an ad agency called Kane Advertising.

Hite, then 17, served as an assistant to the agency's two account executives. Morris used his mechanical art skills to prepare finished ads for the account men. He suggested the art layouts, wrote headlines. He'd seen how to do it in *Printer's Ink*.

But Kane Advertising, as do all small agencies, had its

ups and downs. When business temporarily dried up, agency owner Leon Kane had no choice but to cut his payroll. He fired everyone save for Mrs. Kane and Morris Hite. "I don't know why he didn't fire me, too, unless it was because I worked cheaper than the others," recalled Morris. "But Mr. Kane said he would have to take me off salary, $30 a week. He said that we'd divide up everything the agency made." Half of nothing is nothing, of course.

One day as Morris sat alone at the ad agency, an entrepreneur named S.E.J. Cox walked in. Hite could immediate sense in Cox, the president of Universal Oil and Gas Co., a take-charge personality not unlike that of his Uncle Boone. He took an immediate liking to the visitor, who seemed to be in search of help writing advertisements. "He asked me to go to work for him, and I said sure. I didn't even ask him how much he'd pay," said Hite.

Cox didn't pay well, but he offered priceless experience. With the Oklahoma oil boom at its peak, promoters like Cox raced around lining up investors for their drilling ventures. Cox, a former English professor, asked artist/writer Morris to assist in producing a booklet called "Why Investors Lose in Oil." The principal reason could be traced to their failure to participate with Universal Oil and Gas, naturally.

Like Eugene Arnett before him, S.E.J. Cox had a way with words that moved people to action. Hite carefully studied Cox's manner of salesmanship: the come-ons, the promises of benefits, the calls to action. "He was the best writer I'd ever encountered," said Morris.

Through his affiliation with Cox, Hite met many of the business leaders of Oklahoma City, including former governor Jack Walton, who served as chairman of Universal Oil. The contacts proved indispensable when in 1930, 19-year-old Morris Hite opened his own ad agency. Drawing on his experience with Cox, Morris wrote direct mail promotions for other oil and gas promoters. He lined up his first full-time account, Farmers Royalty Corporation. The future looked bright.

Or so it seemed until the economic upheaval signaled by the crash on Wall Street in late 1929 began working its way through the Oklahoma economy. By 1930, Oklahoma's oil boom subsided. Fewer and fewer people had money to invest in new drilling projects. Or anything else.

Hite's advertising business suffered. When sales slow down, businessmen typically react by cutting their ad spending. His business card read "Morris Hite. Advertising Illustration and Layout . . ." and listed an office in the Oklahoma Savings Building, but by 1931 he was doing anything to make a buck. One of his schemes he called "The Culture Company," a mail-order business in which he sold booklets with come-on titles like "Actor's Appearance Secrets" for thirty cents a copy.

Hard times, indeed.

Morris also began promoting amateur boxing contests. He paid $30 a week to rent the Market Square Arena on Friday nights and staged a series of 4-round matches. Tickets sold for 75 cents. Hite, who had boxed a bit himself until suffering a broken nose in the ring, stayed outside the squared circle and hustled tickets. The *Daily Oklahoman* described Hite as "a youthful promoter and local boy."

Fortunately for Hite, in the mid-1930s another character entered his life. He hooked up with R.O. Burbridge, the owner/operator of "University of Tours," based in Kansas City, Missouri. Burbridge offered education-on-wheels. He'd obtained the charter to a defunct university in Georgia, acquired some second-hand Greyhound buses and tried to market summer bus tours. Under Burbridge's program, high school teachers could earn college credits while they traveled throughout the United States.

Burbridge had a problem with salesmanship, which Morris saw at once when he reviewed the sales literature for University of Tours. Burbridge's copy contained numerous religious references and quotations from the Bible. Hite asked why.

"I've got a problem because if you check me out at the bank I don't look too good," confessed Burbridge. "I want people to believe I'm honest and this writing is the only way I know how."

"Don't worry, let me handle this," said Morris. He rewrote his new client's copy, replacing the religious tone with a promise of excitement and romance.

Would You Like To Make $25 to $50 More in Salary? Thrill To Sparkling Romance? Meet Fascinating New Friends? Now . . . The Rapturous Enjoyment of Travel As Known By The Rich Is Made Available To YOU By This Scientific Travel Plan wrote Hite.

"A school teacher who might take one of your tours doesn't want to go to a camp meeting," Morris told Burbridge. "She wants to have a good time."

In recalling his direct mail writing for University of Tours, Hite observed, "This was a textbook case for the selling game, because practically all sales are made first on an emotional response, then on a rational judgment. I sold [Burbridge] on this approach and we really racked 'em in. We loaded those buses."

The bus business helped build Hite's confidence in his abilities as a persuasive communicator. So did his subsequent success with a real estate development company in Oklahoma City. Billington Lumber Co. had built a group of spec houses that sat idle, saddled with $3,500 to $4,000 price tags. The builder bought heavy space in the Oklahoma City newspapers but couldn't attract any prospective buyers.

Enter Hite. Morris paid the builder a visit and convinced him that the selling effort should be based on a direct mail campaign rather than newspapers. Hite had just the right sales message, too.

"What I did was build a list of people who were renting duplexes and apartments at $30 or $35 a month. I wrote them letters that made the appeal 'If you are paying $35 or more per month in rent, you are buying a home for somebody else.' I wrote and sent a series of three letters based on that idea and they really pulled. We got rid of those houses right quick."

The University of Tours and buy-not-rent direct mail efforts put meat on the table for Morris and his new wife, the former Ann Bell. They had been married in January 1934, having met at a boarding house in Oklahoma City.

Morris' income tax records for 1936 indicate a man on his way up. He listed his occupation as a commercial artist and reported gross receipts of $3,270 and net profit of $2,225. Additionally, he had earned $1,050 doing freelance artwork for Graham-Herwig ad agency. The Hites were a two-car family, Morris deducting business mileage on both a '34 Ford Coupe and a '36 Ford Sedan.

By the beginning of 1937, having just turned 26 years old, Morris set his sights on a new advertising horizon—Dallas. He'd handled his share of dreamers and schemers. He wanted a chance at some real clients.

CHAPTER SEVEN

"I THOUGHT I COULD WRITE A BETTER AD, DIRECT A BETTER LAYOUT, MAKE A BETTER SALES PRESENTATION THAN ANY SON OF A BITCH WHO CAME DOWN THE PIKE."—MORRIS HITE

Morris Hite's plan to relocate to Dallas represented a bold move for someone born on the north side of the Red River. As is often true between border states, a natural rivalry existed between Oklahoma and Texas. Many an Oklahoman would sooner live in hell than live in Texas.

But in the 1930s, when sustained drought turned the state's pastures of plenty into a gigantic dust bowl, Oklahomans began a massive exodus. Many Okies headed west to California—John Steinbeck's fictional Joad family among them—and not a small number went south to Texas.

Hite's motivation for leaving Oklahoma City had to do with advertising, not agriculture. He needed to hitch on to some growing accounts. In Oklahoma, the ad business had been withering.

Morris had developed some new package designs for Dr Pepper. When he showed the ideas to his friend Vernon Beals, who ran a local printing company and used Hite for freelance artwork, Beals suggested to Hite that he show his stuff to the company's ad agency, Tracy-Locke-Dawson. Portfolio in hand, Morris paid a visit to Dallas in the spring of '37. He found Tracy-Locke-Dawson's offices on the top floor of the Majestic Theater on Elm Street downtown. He met with Ray Locke, one of the co-principals, and showed off his wares. (Toting a portfolio into ad agencies is a lot like selling Fuller-Brushes door-to-door: I got this. I got that. See anything you like?)

"Ray and I hit it off beautifully. He was fascinated with my portfolio and case histories. We talked for three or four hours, long after the office had closed, and he finally offered me a job."

Sort of. Locke's letter to Hite came with a caveat. Wrote Locke: "If we find at any time after 30 days and before 90 days that things are not going to work out to our mutual satisfaction, I would like to feel free, and to have you feel free, to say so and call it quits. While we do not anticipate this eventuality, I am suggesting it to relieve both of us of possible embarrassment in case it does not turn out that way."

Locke offered Morris $300 a month. "If you are willing to come down here on that salary, we are willing to gamble with you," he wrote.

Hite didn't hesitate in wiring back his acceptance. He packed his belongings, his wife and his 73-year-old father into the Ford Coupe and headed south. Dallas or bust.

"We figured he'd catch on in Dallas," said Vernon Beals, who later founded Beals Advertising. "Morris was a talented fellow to begin with. He was born with a good brain. We knew he was on his way."

With the work ethic learned early on in Anadarko, the wisdom imparted by a Jersey cow, the exposure to great persuaders like Arnett and Cox, and accumulated experience of running his own shop, the Morris Hite who signed on at Tracy-Locke seemed awfully sure of himself. Call it cocky.

"I was brash," he admitted. "When I arrived in Dallas I was a 26-year-old who thought he could write a better ad, direct a better layout, make a better sales presentation than any son of a bitch who came down the pike. I was a red-hot artist, account man, bill collector, you name it."

Like the agency's two newest employees, Tracy-Locke-Dawson had roots in Oklahoma City. The agency had been formed there in 1913 as Southwestern Advertising Co. It began as a partnership between Shelley Tracy, the ad manager for Williamson-Halsell-Frazier wholesale grocers and Raymond Locke, a former newspaper adman in Kansas who operated Locke Advertising Agency.

Between them, they had the advertising bases covered. Tracy had natural sales ability and an instinct for marketing. Locke possessed a creative flair. The agency landed its first client, Louis Brand Coffee, and took off.

Over the next five years, Southwestern Advertising Co. expanded rapidly, setting up a network of satellite offices in Tulsa, Wichita, and Dallas. Even the interruption of World War I didn't stop the agency's growth. Though Uncle Sam called away most of the agency's account men, Ray Locke, who suffered from a congenital arthritic condition and was physically unfit for service, brought in new advertising recruits to maintain client service. Among the newcomers during 1918 was Joe M. Dawson, a future partner-to-be.

Shelly Tracy served for six months as state chairman of the American Red Cross effort, during which he created a slogan the Red Cross subsequently adopted for use worldwide: *All You Need Is A Heart and A Dollar*. Tracy later enlisted in Officers Candidate School and received his commission shortly before Armistice Day in 1918.

By 1920, Southwestern Advertising Co.'s payroll had reached 60 and the agency's future growth seemed boundless. But a depression in 1920 dealt a near-deadly blow to the agency. The economic downturn squeezed profits of many businesses and exposed Tracy-Locke to a common ad agency disease called "Too Much Too Soon" syndrome.

The Dallas office, which opened that same year, had aggressively scheduled business without properly managing its accounts receivable. Printing technologies being what they were at the time, advertisers were required to buy space several months prior to publication dates. The ad agency would pay the publication, then turn around and collect from the client, earning its commission.

Tracy-Locke's Dallas office had contracted for national advertising space for two clients that went bankrupt virtually overnight. The failed clients left Southwestern Advertising Co. owing $60,000 for ads that had already run in various newspapers, magazines and other media.

Tracy, Locke and Dawson didn't have $60,000 between them. Not even close. "The agency was insolvent," recalled Hite, who first heard the details during his first interview with Ray Locke. "They owed more money than they had on hand. Now a lesser outfit would have folded up, or perhaps would have sought protection in the bankruptcy courts, but those guys were determined to work things out another way.

"Instead of taking protection under bankruptcy laws, they told their creditors, 'We're not taking bankruptcy. We'll pay you off in full, plus interest, if you just give us time.' They signed personal notes for all the obligations owed to media. Then they slashed their own salaries to the bare minimum and operated as frugally and efficiently as they could. When they made money they used it to pay the agency's debts. It took them until 1927, but they paid off all their debts."

The manner in which the agency principals had handled adversity established the agency's reputation with the media throughout the Southwest. "When I joined up in 1937, the agency had made a reputation for paying off its debts in full, plus interest," said Hite. "Oldtimers in the media business still talked about the integrity those guys had shown."

In 1921, as Southwestern Advertising Co. began the long road back, Shelley Tracy and Joe Dawson began operating out of the Southwestern Life building in Dallas. Later they moved to the Simpson-Whiteman building before leasing space in the Majestic Theatre in 1925. Ray Locke remained in Oklahoma City until 1923, when he closed the Oklahoma City office and moved to Dallas. The agency reincorporated in 1923 as Tracy-Locke-Dawson and began writing a new chapter.

Ironically, an agency connection back in Oklahoma would ensure its future success. In 1922, Southwestern Advertising had signed up Marland Oil Refinery in Ponca City, Oklahoma. Marland sold out to Continental Oil in Denver in 1929, and Tracy-Locke-Dawson opened a service office in the Mile High City. Upon arriving in Denver, however, the agency discovered that Continental already had its own agency. An outfit called McCann-Erickson.

Continental's management decided to keep both agencies on board for 90 days and may the best shop win. In this instance, the best shop was Tracy-Locke-Dawson. According to Hite, the agency did some of its best work in advertising Conoco gasoline and motor oil, and in 1933, when the J.P. Morgan family interests bought Continental, Tracy-Locke-Dawson moved with the account to New York.

Shelley Tracy and Joe Dawson opened the agency's Manhattan office at 22 East 40th Street. Many of the agency's most experienced account men—Howard McGhee, H.E. Hendrick, James Clark, Mario Messina, James McPhail and Marshall Roland—also relocated from Dallas.

Ray Locke stayed put in Dallas, where he handled the account of Dr Pepper. Locke headed an office staff that included V.M. (Wally) Wallace, C.B. Wakeley, Howell Robins and Monty Mann.

New York soon became the agency's glamour office. Even with the country still deep in Depression, New York pulsated with opportunity. Shelley Tracy and Dawson feverishly began signing up new accounts. *Newsweek* magazine, Jarman Shoes, Mallory Hats, Hickock Belts, Freuhoff

Trailers all came aboard. The energetic Dawson proved to be a particular whiz at selling new business.

"When I joined the agency in 1937," said Hite, "the New York office was going full bore. They'd put together an impressive account list. The agency had become one of the 25 largest agencies in the whole industry."

In Dallas, by contrast, Locke centered his activities around the Dr Pepper account. "Ray Locke was so wrapped up in that one account he neglected everything else. He wasn't going out calling on new accounts. Of course, with his physical limitations, that was difficult for him to do and probably somewhat embarrassing as well," Morris said.

Locke's arthritic condition made it impossible for him to sit down. He worked behind a specially built-up desk in a saddle chair that gave him support in a half-sitting position. Locke fawned over Dr Pepper, an account he'd nurtured since 1926. Locke worked closely with J. B. O'Hara, one of the company's pioneers who made Dr Pepper a regional brand and set the stage for its ultimate success nationally.

Agency copywriter Erle Racey penned the slogan "Drink A Bite To Eat" to which Ray Locke added "At 10-2-4 O'Clock." Locke and Racey based the creative strategy on research studies from Johns Hopkins University that showed a person's energy level dips at several regular intervals during the day. The agency positioned the non-cola, fruit-flavored drink not as refreshment but as an energy boost. One that needed to be consumed three times a day, yet.

"Other than Dr Pepper, which accounted for maybe 70 or 80 percent of the business, the Dallas office was a sick operation. It was going to hell in a handbasket," Hite recalled. "The guy I reported to drank too much and chased the skirts. But that gave me a real opportunity to make a mark for myself by selling some new accounts."

Hite brought in accounts like Neuhoff, a meat packing co., Tex-Tan, makers of men's belts, Geophysical Services Inc., the forerunner of Texas Instruments, Otis Pressure Controls. "None of them was a particularly significant advertiser, but it gave the shop a bit of a boost."

Advertising agencies have three ways to grow: through sales increases of existing clients that produce larger ad budgets; through attracting new clients and their ad budgets; through acquiring other ad agencies and their clients. Most agency growth results from the first two methods, though in the late 1980s, acquisitions and mergers have been the way of the adworld.

Watching existing accounts grow can be rewarding, but risky. Not only are failure rates high, but often when a growing company achieves success it takes on new trappings of wealth and power. A new corporate headquarters. A new country club affiliation. A new ad agency.

Many an adman, Morris Hite included, has watched helplessly as an advertiser he's helped nurture decides to go Big Time. An ad agency's size often is used against it by ex-clients as a justification for moving to larger agencies. Not that it makes good business sense, but it's a documented pattern.

By 1938, Morris was making a name for himself in Dallas, building a network of business contacts around the city. Word filtered back to Raymond Locke about the young account man's zeal. Morris already worked on the Borden, Imperial Sugar and Mrs Baird's accounts but Locke, naturally, tried to reassign Hite the Dr Pepper account. Put the best people on the best account, right?

"It was fortunate that the first time I made a presentation at Dr Pepper I upset them pretty badly because I didn't agree with a lot of things they were doing. They called the agency and requested that Ray Locke never let that young man come back there again."

That was just fine with Hite. He knew that someone at

the agency had to go out and land some new accounts and he seemed the most eager and willing.

Hite could see a rift developing between New York and Dallas over new business development. Tensions didn't ease when Shelley Tracy decided to leave the agency in 1939. That left Dawson and Locke, polar opposites when it came to their philosophies about new business. A showdown seemed inevitable.

In 1940, Morris Hite signed on a small manufacturer of men's pants, called the Haggar Co. He'd made an appointment with the company's founder, J.M. Haggar, and discovered they had a common background in, of all places, Oklahoma. Haggar had received much of his training in business working in the town of Bristow, Oklahoma.

Haggar, an emigrant from Lebanon, embodied the attributes Hite valued most: directness, resourcefulness and consuming ambition. The clothing salesman could see the same qualities mirrored by the young account executive. They clicked.

Haggar's oldest son, Ed, a graduate of Notre Dame, had joined the family business in 1939 and assumed responsibilities for advertising and marketing. Together with Morris Hite, Ed Haggar mapped out a plan for his father's company to begin advertising its name nationally. The idea struck the company's sales force as bizarre: nobody except Arrow shirts advertised menswear; certainly nobody advertised pants.

But Haggar and Hite could see a new clothing category waiting to be created. Leisure wear. They collaborated on magazine ads that said "the trend is to trousers." Rather than wearing suit pants without the jacket, or work pants for the plant, American men received encouragement to buy spare pants just to sit around in. Suit pants wear out; work pants stain the furniture; try slacks (so called by Ed Haggar because men were to wear them during their "slack" time).

Haggar's ad program began modestly, with ads in trade publications like Daily News Record and Men's Wear, but with Hite's guidance and encouragement Haggar soon began buying schedules in *Esquire, Look* and *Collier's*. The spadework in the early 1940s set the stage for Haggar to become the nation's leading manufacturer of men's pants and expand into full lines.

By the early 1940s, Morris Hite had leapfrogged to the No. 2 job in Dallas. He had won the confidence of his advertising accounts. Nothing stood in his way to success. Nothing but another World War.

CHAPTER EIGHT

"I WAS JUST MAKING A CONTRIBUTION TO THE AGENCY AND UNCLE SAM SENDS ME GREETINGS. I ENDED UP BEING THE OLDEST SON OF A BITCH IN THE SERVICE AND LIKED TO NEVER GOT OUT."—MORRIS HITE

Shortly after Japan's surprise attack on Pearl Harbor pulled the United States into World War II, Morris Hite knew he'd be wise to prepare for military service. Thirty-one years old, married but with no children, he knew he wouldn't be in the first wave of draftees. Younger men and unmarried men went first. But Morris also knew that if the war didn't end quickly, sooner or later his number would come up with Uncle Sam.

A commission with the U.S. Marine Corps—the Marines were looking for a few good admen to help them recruit volunteers—presented one alternative. Morris turned it down, however, setting his sights on becoming a Navy pilot. He began taking flying lessons in Dallas at Mustang Airfield. One of his business contacts, a sugar broker named Bob Armstrong whom Hite knew through the Imperial Sugar ad account, checked out Hite on his first solo flight.

"Morris called me one day in late '42 and said 'Bob, I'm having a little trouble learning to fly. Will you help me out?'" recalled Armstrong, the son of Oscar Armstrong, Imperial Sugar's sales manager. "I told him 'Morris, I've never seen a man yet who couldn't fly an airplane. I want you to show me what you're doing wrong and we'll get it all straightened out.'"

They arranged to meet at an airfield south of Dallas one Sunday morning, and Morris arrived showing the effects of too much Saturday night honky-tonkin'. Despite his hangover, Hite told Armstrong, "Hell, Bob, let's get going," and climbed aboard the Piper Cub.

"We went up and it was obvious that Morris hadn't received the best flight instruction," said Armstrong. "No one had communicated to him exactly what you're trying to accomplish when you're landing an airplane. I showed him, and within an hour or so he had it all down."

Hite started accumulating enough solo hours to qualify for a private pilot's license, which he needed to be eligible for Navy flight school. But to receive his Navy commission, Morris also had to pass a written exam that included one section on math.

Hite had no trouble working with numbers. He could quickly figure Tracy-Locke-Dawson's 15 percent commission on an ad placed with media or compute quarterly sales projections for Borden milk. But being a high school dropout, he lacked exposure to formal math classes and felt anxious and unsure about what the Navy's exam would require.

Luckily for him, Morris found a tutor at Tracy-Locke-Dawson. The agency's business manager, John Wellenkamp, had previously been a high school math teacher. Wellenkamp agreed to instruct Hite in the principles of algebra and geometry and give him a refresher course in math. For weeks during the summer and fall of 1942, they stayed after-hours at the agency's office cramming Hite's head full of equations and parabolas.

Morris proved to be a quick study. He aced the math test and gained acceptance into the pilot program, receiving his commission as a Navy officer. He flew Mustang trainers at Henley Field near Grand Prairie, Texas, and took additional training in Kansas and Nebraska before being assigned to Callendar Field in New Orleans in 1943.

Hite became a flight instructor at Callendar Field, something of a hazardous duty assignment. He witnessed the death of several students and instructors, principally caused by students "freezing on the stick" during a dive. The training accidents began to unnerve Morris. Finally, on a night exercise calling for several planes to fly in formation, Morris' student pilot became disoriented and clipped the wing of another plane. Hite didn't react quickly enough to prevent the collision and was forced to crash land the plane.

The brush with death shook Morris badly. He checked into the Monteleone Hotel in the New Orleans' French Quarter with a sackful of whiskey under his arm and didn't emerge for three days. When he reported back to his unit, Morris was told that "for the good of the service" he should surrender his commission. He walked out of the Navy, turned a corner on Canal Street and noticed an Army recruiting office. He walked in.

Hite received a commission as an Army lieutenant and in late 1943 entered a celestial navigation school being conducted on Lake Pontchartrain near New Orleans. He became part of the water division of the Army Transportation Corps, which Gen. Douglas MacArthur employed in his Pacific campaigns.

Hite received orders to report to Seattle in early 1944. There he went through several weeks of training off Puget Sound with the 347th Boat Co. He shipped out to the Pacific aboard an LCM (Landing Craft Medium) and in the ensuing months operated primarily out of ports around New Guinea. Hite's vessel carried amphibious assault troops ashore during the United States' island-hopping offensive in the southwest Pacific theater. He earned three battle stars during Gen. MacArthur's campaign to reclaim the Philippines.

By the spring of 1945, Hite had been promoted to captain and reassigned to a seagoing tugboat designated LT352. The 123-foot, 900-ton vessel hauled ordinance, heavy equipment and supplies to the front lines during the island assaults.

Hite had two Texas buddies he'd met back in navigation school in New Orleans, Don Luce and Tom Yost, as his first officer and navigator. They were known to break out a Texas flag, with its lone star, whenever LT352 sailed under colors. The rest of Morris' 21-man crew included a mixture of Americans, Aussies, New Zealanders and Filipinos.

When Hite and his crew weren't fighting the war, they were fighting boredom. They engaged in enough hijinks to have rated their own episode of the early 1960s TV show "McHale's Navy." They'd sail into port and collect their food supplies and cigarette rations on one day, then sail in and collect another tugboat's supplies the next. They were magicians at paperwork, cutting orders and requisitions, and as a result the men aboard LT352 seldom wanted for food or drink or smokes.

On one occasion, Hite's tug received orders to tow out an old liberty ship blocking a harbor so that the ship could be torpedoed by a PT Boat.

"The PT skipper and I got together and came up with an ingenious plan," Hite recalled. "The torpedos he was carrying had several gallons of pure alcohol in them, so we decided to dismantle one torpedo and drain the alcohol out and divide it between his boat and mine. Then we sank the ship with the other torpedo.

"On our report, we explained that the first torpedo missed the target and we had to use the second one. Mixed with grapefruit juice or pineapple juice or just about any kind of juice, that alcohol made great booze. We had quite a party."

Hite skippered his ship with a philosophy of maximum effort and minimum military protocol. He insisted that everything on board LT352 be kept squeaky clean with spit and polish, but he purposely allowed the tugboat's exterior to run down. Morris knew inspection teams and Army brass tended to stay away from tugs with old tires hanging off the side and other signs of dishevelment. The inspectors and the brass didn't especially want to get their hands dirty, which was just fine with Hite.

One of the members of Morris' crew hailed from Reno, Nevada and was no stranger to a deck of cards. After he cleaned out the other crew members in a couple of poker games, Hite realized he had a serious problem developing.

So Morris channeled the man's talents into other directions. As LT352 came into port, Hite would do reconnaissance to find out where the big money poker games were being played. More often than not, the game would be scheduled for the officer's club. The card shark happened to be an enlisted man, but no problem. He'd borrow a uniform from Luce or Yost, and Hite would go along as his bodyguard. The card shark's winnings went into a kitty the crew split. Black market sales of cigarettes, whiskey, sirloin steaks, and other supplies that LT352 just happened to have in abundance added to the kitty.

When the card shark gained a reputation around the Philippines naval bases, Hite took to disguising the Reno Kid with a wig and moustache and kept him going. His propensity for coming home awash with cash helped pay for some memorable parties when LT352's crew took liberty on shore.

Hite's style of leadership—firm but not harsh—matured during his years at sea. "He was one of the finest natural leaders I've ever known," said Luce. "He didn't tell you to do anything, he *asked*, and he never asked a soldier to do anything that he himself wasn't prepared to do. If anyone was going to take the risk, it would be Morris first."

LT352 remained away from the heavy combat. Once a

kamikaze pilot tried to ram the tugboat, narrowly missing. Strafing by enemy aircraft claimed several lives. More life-threatening than the Japanese to the crew of LT352 were the three typhoons they had to endure. Being on board a tugboat in a typhoon couldn't be called ideal—a cruiser or aircraft carrier would have been preferable, thank you—but fortunately LT352 had weighty tows on their lines that helped keep them from capsizing.

"The closest call I had was after the war was over," said Hite. "In September of 1945, we got caught in a typhoon between Okinawa and Yokohama. Our convoy broke up and we lost contact with everybody in these 100-foot-high swells. It was like riding a giant roller coaster."

Hite tied himself down in the wheelhouse, battened down the hatches and ordered everyone to stay below deck. "We finally made it to a little port at the northern tip of the Philippines," he said. "I went straight to the officers' club for a few snorts."

Hite also had a few snorts one night when he and Luce had taken a tow up to Yokohama. He was awakened early in the morning by a rattling noise in their hotel room.

"D. Luce. You awake?" Morris whispered.

Luce groggily answered in the affirmative.

"What'd we have to drink last night?" asked Hite.

"I dunno," Luce mumbled. "What's it matter?"

"Look up yonder," said Hite, pointing to a light fixture swinging over their beds. "Whatever we had's making that thing swing. We're going to need some more of it to to make it stop."

No sooner had the words escaped Morris' lips than the tremor they felt turned into an earthquake. It scared them more than any combat duty they'd seen.

Not all of Morris' memories from his days in the Pacific were pleasant ones. Once, disembarking from a small ship-to-shore craft in Manila, he suffered a serious injury to his leg. He got his leg squashed between the side of the boat and the pier, severing a tendon and causing a deep wound. Later, a gangrene-like fungus set in, hobbling him for months. The back pains that bothered him later in life were also exacerbated by the jarring life aboard a tugboat.

Morris also suffered a broken heart. He received a "Dear John" letter from home. His wife's confession that she no longer loved him didn't come as a total surprise. The Hites had been having marital problems long before Morris shipped out overseas. Still, alone at sea, thousands of miles from home, Hite had too much time to brood about his personal life.

"It was a real tough period for Morris," recalled Tom Yost. "Luce and I tried to keep him cheered up. I guess we were instrumental in helping him keep his grip." Plenty of booze helped, too.

In late 1945 and early 1946, the three buddies on LT352 gave some serious thought to staying in the Pacific Basin. As Hite had written in a letter to Jerry Moffett, one of the account men at Tracy-Locke, on May 30, 1945: "There have been times when I have considered not coming back. I have even considered staying in the Philippines," he wrote. "I believe there will be some good business opportunities over here during the reconstruction."

Hite, Luce and Yost looked into operating a barge line in the Philippines between Leyte and Manila. There was no transportation between the islands and buying the equipment from the U.S. Army would have been simple. The Army had all kinds of surplus to unload, tugboats included.

They also talked about operating a barge line in China. In late 1945, LT352 took a tow from Yokohama to Shanghai. Hite found Shanghai intriguing, because he could see the long-term potential for any businessman, especially a natural promoter like himself, getting in on the ground floor of China's economic development. Unfortunately, he could also see the Communist Chinese posing a serious threat to Chiang Kai-shek's government. So despite giving serious thought to setting up a barge business along the Yangtze River, Morris finally opted to head back to the USA.

He also thought of taking his talents back east, trying his hand at a New York agency. The time seemed as good as any. He had no family to speak of, his father having died in Dallas in November 1942 and his wife having fallen in love with another man. Morris Hite was 35 years old and a little uncertain about his future.

Leaving Tom Yost to knock around in Manila, Morris Hite and Don Luce headed home in May 1946. They sailed to San Francisco in the hold of a liberty ship, a 30-day voyage where all the returning troops on board stayed drunk or seasick. When they reached port, they headed straight for a barber shop, where they got a haircut and shave. They went to a clothing store and bought some civvies, throwing away their khaki uniforms. Then they headed for a bar.

After five days of revelry in San Francisco, Hite and Luce boarded a troop train to San Antonio and reported to Fort Sam Houston for out-processing. Their pockets full of cash from their share of LT352's kitty, they bribed a couple of ex-GIs to wait in line for them and holed up in a downtown San Antonio hotel on a three-day binge. Then they were free to go. As a parting gesture, the Army promoted Morris Hite to major. Uncle Sam squared his pay and handed him a train ticket to Dallas.

Hite came back to a much different agency than the one he'd left. While Morris had gone to sea, the agency had gone to seed. The friction between the Dallas and New York offices had resulted in Ray Locke and Joe Dawson having split acrimoniously. The Dallas office had been reincorporated in 1943 as Tracy-Locke Co. Ray Locke, who owned all the agency, kept the name Tracy out of respect to his first partner; the name Dawson he never wished to see or hear again.

Locke had spent the war years in the same manner as the pre-war years, concentrating on Dr Pepper. Hite soon saw the other accounts had suffered as a result. "When I got back, I found that the organization had really deteriorated. It was a pretty sad situation. My three old favorite accounts, Borden, Imperial Sugar, and Mrs Baird's —you'd have to add Haggar as my fourth favorite—were restless and considering leaving. They were terribly unhappy with the service they were being given. Some of the account service people hired during the war years were a collection of misfits and drunks. All in all, it was a hectic time."

Hite began by reestablishing relations with his key accounts. Together with Bob Armstrong, his flying teacher, Morris helped Imperial Sugar solidify its base of support by focusing on a new sales strategy. Hite and Armstrong mapped out a plan and took it to Imperial's management in Sugar Land.

During World War II, as part of the conservation effort to reduce railroad shipments, the U.S. government established zoning regulations on the distribution of various commodities. As they applied to sugar refineries, the zoning regulations gave Imperial Sugar Co. almost exclusive distribution within Texas. Where the company had roughly 30 percent of the consumer market before the war, it had almost 100 percent during 1942-46. (The same regulations prohibited Imperial from selling outside Texas.)

Hite and Armstrong thought Imperial should protect its market dominance in Texas by reducing its sales territory and redeploying its sales force throughout the Lone Star State. Being the principal player in a growing market seemed a sound strategy to both men.

Armstrong, who succeeded his father as sales manager, immediately launched an intensive campaign within the grocery trade, urging wholesalers to carry only one line of sugar. Hite often accompanied Armstong on the sales calls, chiming in with assurances that his advertising would create consumer demand for the Imperial brand.

"Don't worry, we'll handle the advertising end of it," Morris would say. And Tracy-Locke did indeed support the Imperial effort with heavy newspaper and radio advertising in local Texas markets, which helped Imperial entrench itself as Texas' leading brand of sugar.

Tracy-Locke also aided the effort by creating a heavy mail order volume for Imperial. The agency helped create recipes and cookbooks that consumers could obtain by sending in the red "Pure Cane Sugar" tag from a bag of Imperial. Hite also created goodwill for Imperial Sugar by arranging its sponsorship of a popular radio program featuring a vocal group called The Stamps Baxter Quartet.

Hite's second move was to start going out with Ray Locke's secretary, Caroline Roemer. Caroline's father, Jerry Roemer, had been an account man at Tracy-Locke-Dawson back in the 1920s, before failing health had forced him to resign and move to Colorado.

After Jerry Roemer's death in 1935, the family moved back to Dallas. Caroline Roemer finished North Dallas H.S. in 1942 and began working as a secretary at Southwestern Life. She later left the insurance company to work for Walker, Austin & Waggener, a stock brokerage firm.

In the spring of '46, Ray Locke hired Caroline to be his secretary. A few months later, she met Morris Hite. The first time she saw him he was standing in front of a mirror in the lobby of the agency, putting on a Tex-Tan belt. She thought he was cute, even if his clothes were a bit ill-fitting.

"I sure would like to go out with him," Caroline thought to herself, and someone at the agency read her mind. Ernie Lovan, one of the account men, invited Caroline over for a backyard cookout. He invited Morris, too.

By the fall of 1946, Morris Hite and Caroline Roemer were an item. And on February 8, 1947, they exchanged wedding vows.

"My mother always told me never to marry an adman because of all the work that's involved," said Caroline. "They work 24 hours a day, plus Saturday and Sunday. She said 'don't say I didn't warn you.'

"But I knew Morris. I knew I would come second in his life behind his work. At times it made me awfully mad, but I accepted it. I've always said it's better to be married to someone who loves his work and is gone quite a bit than it is to be married to a 9-to-5 guy who's bored with his life," she said.

Shortly after Mr. and Mrs. Morris Hite celebrated their first anniversary in 1948, Tracy-Locke celebrated its 35th. Ray Locke told a reporter from *The Dallas Morning News*: "Next to Christianity, advertising is the greatest force in the world. And I say that without sacrilege or disrespect. Advertising makes people discontented. It makes them want things they don't have. Without discontent, there is no progress, no achievement."

In 1949, Locke learned more about discontent than he cared to. A group of investors from St. Louis wrested control of Dr Pepper away from J.B. O'Hara, Locke's close friend and ally. With control of the company, the new ownership chose to exercise its new authority and act discontented with the way the business was being run.

Said Hite: "Like new owners generally do, they looked around and decided to change everything. The result was Tracy-Locke got fired. It broke Ray's heart, since he put his life into building that account. It really crushed him, even though the circumstances were beyond his control."

A dispirited Ray Locke stayed in the job for a few months, but he could barely go through the motions of being an adman. In March 1950 he announced his retirement from the company he had co-founded with Shelley Tracy. In a formal statement the agency issued, Locke said:

"For all these 37 years we have subscribed to the philosophy: 'Advertising must pay its way and pay a profit.'

Hence we have prospered to the same degree that our clients have prospered. This has paid off for our clients and for our advertising agency and for me. I shall part with my associates with regret, but I have confidence that they will carry on in the traditions of the firm."

Morris Hite certainly planned to carry on. He immediately went to Republic National Bank and borrowed the money to buy out Ray Locke's interest in the agency. "In retrospect, I don't know why the Republic Bank loaned me money to buy him out," he said. "I had no assets and damn poor prospects."

Hite became Tracy-Locke's new president. Clay Stephenson, who had joined the agency in 1948, succeeded Morris as executive vice president. John Wellenkamp, the vice president/treasurer, added the additional responsibility as general services manager. Hite owned the majority of the Tracy-Locke stock, with Stephenson and Wellenkamp taking small equity positions.

Even as Dr Pepper's exit spelled the end of the founders' participation in Tracy-Locke, it signaled the beginning of a new era. The Morris Hite era.

CHAPTER NINE

"TO HELL WITH A MARKETING PLAN. WHAT WE NEED IS TO MAKE A LIST OF PROSPECTS AND GO CALL ON THEM."—MORRIS HITE

Tracy-Locke's new president had learned from the Dr Pepper saga how an ad agency can become too dependent on a single account. Agency executives who depend on a single client for half or more of their revenues live with constant anxiety of knowing one change of heart can endanger their livelihood.

Which makes ulcers common, and Tagamet the prescription drug of choice, among ad executives.

Changes in client ownership or management often mandate changes in other professional services like legal counsel, outside auditors and ad agencies. Only ad agencies are more vulnerable because few clients put admen on the same professional plane as lawyers and accountants. And agencies are more vulnerable because the agency's work appears for all the world to see and hear—including the chief executive officer's pals at the country club and his wife and family.

When's the last time anyone even knew the auditors screwed up a client's financial reports? But everyone gets to have a say about a company's ad campaign.

As soon as Hite assumed control at Tracy-Locke, he mounted a new business effort. The agency's billings, after Dr Pepper's exit, had fallen to about $1.2 million, meaning Morris would either have to build the account list quickly or reduce the agency's staff. He hated the thought of having to wield the ax.

But before Hite could embark on his new business plan, two more accounts followed Dr Pepper out the door. Morris had scarcely moved into his new office when he received a summons from the ad manager at Republic National Bank, a long-time client. The banker promptly informed Hite of a new direction for the bank's advertising.

"Morris, we're going to split the account three ways," the banker said. "I'm giving you first choice. Tracy-Locke can have the radio, newspaper or the trade portion. Which will it be?"

"You're going to split your account?" roared the adman. "What on earth for?"

"Look, that's the way many advertisers are doing business these days," said the banker. "Take your General Motors, your Procter & Gamble, your . . ."

"For Chrissakes, they're national advertisers with multimillion dollar ad budgets," Morris interjected. "General Motors probably does have enough business to keep three agencies busy. But you folks don't have enough for one agency, let alone three."

The banker didn't budge. He wanted three agencies working on his account. Hite could like it or lump it.

Morris lumped it. Steaming, he returned to his office in the Guardian Life Building and dashed off a letter of resignation to Fred Florence, chairman of the bank.

Exit Republic.

Continental Supply Co. became the next casualty. The circumstances reflected an age-old story in advertising: the account man gets to be so tight with the client ad manager that their personal bond outweighs the bond between the advertiser and its agency.

Had Morris Hite ever elected to leave Tracy-Locke, for example, many of his clients would have followed him. Their loyalties were to Morris first, Tracy-Locke second. This situation also explains why many agencies require executives to sign non-compete or non-steal contracts, though the validity of such contracts might not stand up in court.

"The guy we had working on our Continental Supply account was a drunk," Morris confessed. "Every afternoon about 2:30 or 3:00, he'd go into his office, shut the door and proceed to get tanked.

"And that wasn't the worst of it. When he drank, he'd get on the telephone and start calling our clients, making an absolute ass out of himself. He caused a hell of a lot of grief before we realized what was going on."

Morris had no choice but to fire the account man. But no sooner had he done so than Continental Supply's ad manager stormed in to Hite's office demanding an explanation. Hite saw that the ad manager had no intention of losing his after-hours drinking buddy, that he cared more about good times than good advertising.

"If you sack him, then I'm going too," the ad manager warned.

Hite swallowed hard. "I'm sorry. I have no other choice. He's gone."

So was the ad manager, who kept the account in the hands of his drinking pal.

Exit Continental Supply.

"Here I was, just getting started in business and I had promptly lost two of the best accounts the agency had," said Hite. Luckily, things started to improve.

Hite scored his first success late in 1950 when he won the account of the Rio Grande Valley Citrus Exchange Program, producers of Tex-Sun fruit drinks. Tracy-Locke prevailed in an agency review that included an initial screening process of nearly 50 southern and midwestern agencies and a final showdown that brought representatives of four shops to Weslaco, Texas.

Competitive agency reviews constitute one of the most riveting facets of the advertising business. While some advertisers choose quietly to recruit an agency on a one-to-one basis, many companies, especially the larger ones, prefer to "review" the capabilities of several agencies at once.

The agency review process follows this general pattern: client companies ask prospective agencies to fill out written questionnaires that cover such basic information as agency history, personnel, client lists, staffing on accounts, creative awards, major accomplishments and so forth. Next comes an introductory meeting, a virtual feeling-out process, wherein the client visits the agency's offices and vice versa. Adpeople use the term "chemistry" to describe the result of this feeling out.

The final step in an agency review is the agency pitch. Agencies that remain in the running—usually two or four reach the final phase—put on a formal presentation to showcase their marketing savvy and creative ability. People in the business commonly call these efforts *dog and pony shows.* Theatrical in tone and self-serving in nature, agency pitches represent a last-ditch effort to sell the prospect.

In some agency reviews, those involving megabudgets or highly visible accounts, agencies will incur the expense of creating new TV commercials to win the client. Such work, called "spec creative," costs agencies out-of-pocket money that they hate to have to eat. Hence the unpopularity of reviews in which spec creative is required or even suggested.

Four finalists presented to the Rio Grande Citrus Exchange Program's board of directors, a group of citrus producers. Tracy-Locke went on third, after the board took a lunch break. "We were damned glad not be number one," said Morris. "We went in the number three spot. In a deal like that, where the prospect sits around all day, they usually can't remember who the hell went first."

Morris' style of presentation to prospective clients could be safely called low-key. He sold the steak, not the sizzle. Rather than employing a flashy, gimmicky style—

rather than trying to be somebody he wasn't—Morris Hite looked the prospect in the eye and told it to him straight. What Hite had to say can be summarized as:

Here's your business. Here's what you do, here's what you do well, here's what you need to improve on. Here's how Tracy-Locke can help you make those improvements. This is what we'll do for you if you'll let us. You interested?

Morris stood beside an A-frame easel, on which he placed his flip-chart presentation. Hite loved flip charts. He'd cram each 35" X 45" chart full of figures, and use 50 or 60 charts in his pitch. As he spoke, he'd move his hands to his waist and hook his thumbs inside his belt loops. At times he'd twiddle his fingers on his stomach. At other times, he'd jam his hands into his trouser pockets and jingle his change.

Hite's body language created an effect that can be summarized as: *This guy's obviously relaxed and totally in control. He's warm and open. He doesn't seem the least bit self-conscious about whether his tie is straight or if his fly is wide open. He sounds like he understands the nitty-gritty of our business. He sounds like he knows exactly what we should be doing with our ad dollars. Maybe we oughta hire him.*

Hite had one more technique for winning prospective clients. Written reports. He'd take his staff's market analysis and add to it the independent research Tracy-Locke had conducted. Then he'd toss in some marketing objectives, sales projections, supporting ad campaigns, point-of-sale materials, promotional tie-ins and so on—until he assembled a document that needed to be weighed on fish scales. "I want a presentation that will make their eyes bug out like shrimps," Morris liked to say.

Morris' skills as a new business presenter derived principally from his analytical approach to business. He broke down a prospective client's business into parts and closely probed each for defects. He added market research that identified potential problems or missed opportunities.

Then he turned attention away from Tracy-Locke and toward the prospect.

Too many advertising principals make the mistake in new business presentations of belaboring what the agency will do for the prospect. Call it the "Promises, Promises" approach. Morris Hite knew better. He zeroed in on the prospect's needs that Tracy-Locke researchers and account men had uncovered by digging and digging.

When Morris faced the roomful of Rio Grande Valley farmers who sat on the board of the directors of the advertising co-op, he felt a glint of recognition. These people made their living working the land. They were honest, down-to-earth, good old farm boys just like him. A sense of confidence swept over Hite. He knew they'd relate to him. He knew they'd consider him a *compadre*.

Morris had barely begun Tracy-Locke's pitch when he noticed one farmer seated to his left having a nap attack. His head began to nod and weave and presently, to Hite's amazement, the farmer fell fast asleep.

"Not only did he fall asleep during my pitch," Morris laughed, "but then he started snoring."

Hite had plenty of experience as a public speaker and knew that if he directed his voice at the man and used inflection, he might be able to wake the man up. He tried and tried without success. Who was this guy, Rip Van Winkle?

"Goddamn, it has a helluva distraction," Hite remembered. "I was pretty sore about it, too." But Morris scored major points when he was asked about Tracy-Locke's stipulations about a contract.

"Hell, we don't have a contract. We work with a handshake agreement. We know you're honorable people and so are we. Give us the business and we'll go to work for you and do a good job and you'll be happy. If you're not happy with our work, we wouldn't want you to stay with us anyway."

Hite and Clay Stephenson, who accompanied Morris to Weslaco, returned to the local motel were they'd booked a room for the night. Now they had to sweat out a decision. Ad clients have been known to take days, even weeks, to render a verdict in agency reviews. The Texas fruit farmers, though, didn't dilly-dally.

The phone rang. "Morris, you got the business. Congratulations." The call came from Randy Brooks of Rogers & Smith, another Dallas agency that had pitched the business. The farmers had called the losing agencies first. A nice gesture.

"Thanks, Randy. I still want to hear it from them," said Hite. The phone rang again. "Morris, I'm happy to tell you that Tracy-Locke's got the business," said the Tex-Sun plant manager. "We know you'll do a good job for us."

Morris promised the account would get Tracy-Locke's best effort. He'd see to it himself. But Hite remained curious about one thing:

"Tell me," he said, "You know the fellow who fell asleep when I was talking? Which way did he vote?"

"Hell, Morris," came the reply, "He was your biggest supporter."

The euphoria from winning the Tex-Sun presentation proved to be short-lived. As Tracy-Locke developed the client's marketing plan and started work on its creative, Mother Nature intervened. A winter storm in January 1951 dumped snow and ice on the Texas valley, destroying the entire citrus crop. It would be several seasons before the crop would start to recover and several more years before the Valley people were in a position to advertise. Morris Hite's first new business coup had died on the vine.

Not all of Tracy-Locke's new business efforts in the early years of Hite's helmsmanship met with such ignominious ends. In the spring of 1951, Tracy-Locke put together a milestone introduction for Duncan Coffee Co.

Drawing on Morris Hite's grocery store savvy and Clay Stephenson's coffee expertise, Tracy-Locke almost overnight made Maryland Club coffee the second best-selling brand in Texas.

The Duncan Coffee Co., based in Houston, sold the "Bright and Early" label, which ranked third in coffee sales in Texas behind Folger's and Maxwell House. Duncan also sold a premium brand called Maryland Club to four-star restaurants and country clubs. Maryland Club had no identity with the general public.

Clay Stephenson knew the coffee business from his days as advertising manager of Folger's Coffee in his hometown of Kansas City. Stephenson was an exacting, precise adman who could be extremely demanding on the staff. He'd worked at several ad agencies in New York before joining Tracy-Locke.

Stephenson's polish and sophistication proved formidable when combined with Hite's "aw, shucks" manner. They were at their persuasive best convincing Herschel Duncan, president of Duncan Coffee Co., that they could sell Maryland Club to consumers. And that he should give them $50,000 for a test market in Dallas.

Some of the Duncan sales people, including the ad manager, scoffed at the idea. Maryland Club sold for two or three cents more per pound than regular blends. On a price-sensitive purchase like coffee, the differential would be critical. Shoppers simply wouldn't pay more.

Morris and Clay believed otherwise. Tracy-Locke began by giving the brand a snob appeal, a rare tactic for the times. You might use that approach to sell luxury items, like Cadillacs, but certainly not a volume product like coffee. Not a product bought by people wearing houseslippers, their hair rolled up in curlers. Snob appeal?

The agency positioned the product as upscale, by creating newspaper ads showing Dallas dowagers and socialites drinking Maryland Club coffee in the cozy confines of their Highland Park estates. "Her Coffee Is Maryland Club. . ." read the headlines.

Tracy-Locke also arranged for Maryland Club to be sole sponsor of a local TV show in which Neiman-Marcus showcased some of the new fashions and lines in the famous retail store. Yes, more snob appeal.

Next, Tracy-Locke coined the memorable line "Maryland Club: The Coffee You'd Drink If You Owned All The Coffee In The World." The ad slogan, used in newspaper and radio ads, imbued the product with quality and prestige.

With the Dallas market properly teased, Tracy-Locke scheduled the introduction for Mother's Day weekend. As a promotional tie-in, Tracy-Locke arranged for orchid corsages to be shipped over from Hawaii. Any woman buying 2 pounds of Maryland Club coffee would receive a free orchid corsage. Hite and Stephenson personally called on the grocery chains to be sure they stocked plenty of cases of coffee and ordered a corresponding number of flowers.

The promotion produced a stampede at Dallas grocery stores that fateful Saturday. Shoppers lured by snob appeal came to buy the coffee. Shoppers lured by the orchids bought the coffee. Other shoppers, who saw the hubbub, wanted an orchid, too.

Were grocery store managers going to say no to these women? The day before Mother's Day? No way. Suddenly the whole town was talking about orchid corsages and Maryland Club coffee and grocery store operators began calling Hite and Stephenson at Tracy-Locke demanding more orchids. By mid-afternoon, Hite feared the agency's switchboard might ignite from overheating, so he shut it down and went out to watch some of the chaos he'd created.

"It was the biggest, most successful food promotion that has ever been put on in Dallas," Hite noted. "And as a result in a period of one year, we took Maryland Club, with the sales manager kicking and screaming, from zilch to where it was the number two brand in Texas. We never could catch Folger's, though."

To undergird Maryland Club's popularity, Morris created another reason why shoppers should buy the brand: economy. He created a selling message that said "Since Maryland Club is such a rich blend, you only need to use three-fourths of it to make the same cup of coffee."

In one brilliant stroke, Hite had made a higher-priced brand actually seem to be a lower-price brand.

"Now the housewife could say to her husband, 'Yes, dear, Maryland Club *does* cost a few cents more, but it's so rich it takes 25 percent less coffee to make a pot. We're really saving money.'"

"It was the best of both worlds," said Morris. "We were able to put together both an emotional appeal (sophistication, class) and a rational appeal (economy). Most sales are made for emotional reasons. We like to think we're rational people, but not when it comes to purchasing decisions."

As Maryland Club continued its meteoric rise, Clay Stephenson moved to Houston and opened a branch office. Stephenson wanted to concentrate his energies on the coffee business, his first love.

Tracy-Locke moved to a new headquarters at Cedar Springs and Fairmount in 1953 and the following year the agency opened a second branch office, in New Orleans, after Hite brought in the Regal Beer account.

Regal Beer, at one time the best-selling brand in New Orleans, had slipped behind Falstaff, Jax and Dixie in local sales. It fared even worse throughout Louisiana and Mississippi. Regal's advertising campaign, "Join The Swing To Regal," had produced mediocre results.

A new management team from American Brewing Co. came in and began making changes. Not surprisingly, one of the changes came in advertising. In an agency competition with two Chicago agencies and the New Orleans incumbent, Tracy-Locke emerged the winner.

The decision by Regal's new management to hire an out-of-town ad agency provoked immediate resistance. "New Orleans is a myopically provincial city," Morris explained. "The old-line Catholic, French, Italian and aristocratic Irish families have run things since the days of the Louisiana Purchase. The thinking of the leadership was a mite medieval but they liked things the way they were. And this pull-up-the-drawbridge way of thinking permeated most all levels of society and business."

Hite, therefore, claimed not to be surprised when he received an urgent phone call from Dick McAuliffe, the new president of Regal.

"We've got a problem down here, Morris," said McAuliffe, reading from a letter he'd received from a representative of a graphic arts union. The letter said: *In view of your decision to hire a foreign ad agency, members of our union are going to boycott your product. . . . And urge other union members to boycott it, too.*

McAuliffe, lured away from a position with Pabst in Chicago, had taken steps to improve Regal's performance. He had reorganized the sales force, shored up the product quality, canned the previous advertising and brought in Tracy-Locke. He could see his reclamation project caving in.

"What are we going to do?" McAuliffe asked Hite. Both men knew that union members tend to be large consumers of beer. They also knew no business can afford to anger its best customers.

Morris said he'd think of something. And he did. Then he scheduled a lunch meeting in New Orleans with the bargaining agent of the graphics union.

"We don't know anything about running a union," Morris conceded at the outset of the lunch, "but we assume that you want to do everything you can to create more graphic arts jobs. The more jobs for printers, typographers, engravers, electrotypers and mat workers, the more members you can recruit and the more important your jobs become. Is that about right?"

"That's right," answered the union rep. "That's why we want to keep you guys out and keep the work at home."

"Well let me ask you this," said Morris, "Do you know how the total volume of graphic arts production done in New Orleans compares with that done in Dallas?"

"No, I don't" replied the union rep. "What's that got to do with keeping jobs at home?"

"It has a lot to do with the number of jobs in your industry and the number of members in your unions," said Morris. "Look, even though Dallas is a smaller city than New Orleans, about 430,000 to 570,000, Dallas did almost twice as much graphics work as New Orleans last year."

Hite showed the union man figures he'd compiled from the Department of Commerce and from the Chamber of Commerce in the respective cities.

"Do you know why Dallas generates so many more jobs in graphic arts?" Hite asked. "I'll show you why." He whipped out a copy of the yellow pages in the Dallas telephone directory, showing listings for 112 ad agencies.

"Granted, some of these are small, mom-and-pop operations working off the kitchen table," said Morris. "And some have gone out of business since this was published. But here's what's important to you. Every one of those advertising agencies is selling graphic arts. That's the way they make a living. The graphic arts industry in Dallas has 112 sales organizations out hustling business for them every day, creating work for them."

Hite let the point sink in, then pulled out the yellow pages from the New Orleans directory. "Look how many ad agencies are listed here," Morris said. "Exactly eight. That's why you don't have more graphic arts business.

You've got only eight advertising agencies out selling for you. We're trying to make it nine, and you're trying to keep us out. Hell, you ought to be trying for 112 ad agencies in New Orleans."

The union rep saw Hite's point.

"You're going to open a branch office in New Orleans."

"Yes."

"You'll put local people on your payroll?"

"Everybody except the manager," Hite assured him.

"And the graphic arts work generated by the Regal account will be bought locally?"

"Absolutely."

"That's it," declared the union rep. "The boycott's off."

Tracy-Locke maintained its presence in New Orleans until 1961. "We spent seven long years in the wrong city," said Hite. "About the only good that came out of it was that we sold the Standard Fruit and Steamship Co. account, which was the second largest importer of bananas. They sold bananas under the Cabana brand."

Hite could never accept the provincialism he encountered in New Orleans nor the lack of a progressive posture. "Hell, New Orleans has everything going for it. It's got the Mississippi River, water through the heartland of America. It's the natural gateway to South America through the Gulf of Mexico. It's got a big petrochemical industry. And they've got enough rainfall down there that you can grow anything. Even the telephone poles will sprout.

"But by God, they got a bunch of those old-time people down there that just want to hold everything the way it is. I'll tell you this, if 50 years ago you could have taken the people out of Dallas and put them in New Orleans and put the New Orleans people in Dallas—today New Orleans would be bigger than Chicago and Dallas would be smaller than Waxahachie."

Tracy-Locke's Houston office didn't pan out, either. Clay Stephenson continued to concentrate his efforts on Duncan Coffee Co. to the exclusion of developing new business. Morris, who had seen the same thing happen with Ray Locke, started arguing with Clay about new business development.

In Hite's view, Stephenson over-serviced the Duncan Coffee account. In other words, Clay spent more time working on the business than was justified from the account billings. Ad agencies must carefully balance the amount of work they do for a client against their compensation. Too much service (or too little) can jeopardize a relationship. To provide a basis for determining the proper level of service, employees keep time sheets that show how much service each account receives.

"Clay was giving away too much of his time. He was always betting on the come, projecting his profits out into the hereafter. He was a wealthy man himself and didn't seem to care that much about making money. We had different philosophies of operating the business. I've always felt you're supposed to make money."

When Hite and Stephenson realized how acute their differences were, they struck a deal. In 1959, Clay bought the Houston office of Tracy-Locke and opened Clay Stephenson & Associates. Bob Brown, Richard Brown and Bud Phillips all joined the Stephenson payroll.

While geographic expansion in the 1950s had produced headaches and heartburn for Hite, Tracy-Locke was about to find happiness outside of Dallas.

The fun began in San Antonio in 1960, after Hite sold Pearl Beer. Expansion continued throughout the 1960s, as offices sprang up in Denver, San Francisco and New York. The good times began to roll.

CHAPTER TEN

"HERE'S WHAT WE OUGHT TO DO. NOW GET ME SOME RESEARCH TO PROVE IT."—MORRIS HITE

Tracy-Locke's growth during the 1950s can be attributed in part to its use of research. Whenever Morris Hite paid a visit to a new business prospect, he took with him a business proposal that identified a specific marketing problem (or opportunity) and recommended a solution. He based his proposal on research.

Hite was ahead of his time, at least compared with other ad agencies in the Southwest. Large shops in New York and Chicago had long since set up research departments, and some Madison Avenue agencies like Young & Rubicam had used research methods since the 1920s and 1930s, but in Texas little was being done with research. Joe Belden operated a research company in Dallas, but in the early 1950s Belden concentrated on political polling. Besides Tracy-Locke, no one in Texas applied research to marketing to any significant degree.

Most research efforts by the major ad agencies sought to measure the effectiveness of specific ad campaigns. Agencies attempted to determine what consumers could recall and retain about selling messages. Pre-testing ad copy to see which one among several headline treatments or ad layouts scored best became widely adopted.

Creatives complained research quashed their inspiration. Research inhibited generating new ideas, they argued, since it endorsed existing methods or formulas and discouraged creative risk-taking.

In the 1950s, ad agencies embraced a new concept

called depth motivational research. Motivational research went far beyond asking questions about past ad campaigns; it tried to ascertain from consumers their motivations for buying specific products, information which might lead to the creation of new products, even new categories.

Depth motivational research redirected the focus from the advertiser's product or the advertiser's message to the consumer. Advertisers realized the need to find out more about their customers—why they bought certain products, why they didn't buy others and the underlying reasons for their purchasing decisions. Motivational research provided the sort of clues to understanding consumers that admen had been fishing for all along.

Hite had relied on research long before polls, surveys and focus group studies became fashionable. He assigned prime responsibility for Tracy-Locke's research to two Tracy-Locke employees, Cecil "Bud" Phillips and Elmer "Jack" Taylor. As Hite often joked, "We started doing very questionable research to prove my pre-conceived opinions." In fact, research became a hallmark of Tracy-Locke's account service.

Phillips, a graduate of Southern Methodist University's journalism program, had been hired as a production man by Tracy-Locke in 1949, during the twilight of Ray Locke's era. Phillips had been summoned to Locke's office on his first day at work only to hear the boss tell him: "We don't like college graduates here. Besides, *anybody* can get a degree in journalism."

Jack Taylor came along a few years later. He had an M.B.A. from the University of Texas and had worked at the Bureau of Business Research in Austin before going into the military during the Korean War.

Taylor enjoyed crunching numbers, assimilating data into an intelligible form. He made a good partner for Phillips, who had a knack for data interpretation and persuasive presentations. Hite thought Phillips wrote the best marketing plans in the shop.

Phillips had impressed Morris with his analytical nature. Tracy-Locke prepared holiday season point-of-sale materials for Borden each fall but the number of the press run had been done by guesstimate before Phillips got the job. Leaving nothing to chance, Phillips surveyed the Borden route men as to the exact number of retail stops on their route.

No earth-shattering calculation was needed, just a phone call or two. But Phillips' approach represented the difference between guessing and digging. So simple, yet so advanced.

Hite and Phillips combined talents to conduct an unsolicited study for Mrs Baird's Bread on the use of brown-and-serve dinner rolls. Their effort met with an underwhelming reception.

"Morris," said Roland Baird, one of three brothers who ran the bakery, "instead of trying to do this high-falutin' research stuff why don't you spend more time trying to do some good *advertising* for us?" With that, he tossed the report in the nearest wastebasket.

Undeterred, Hite and Phillips found other research applications for Tracy-Locke clients. Borden's had grown concerned because milk sales in Amarillo lagged considerably behind its other Texas plants. The same ad programs, the same pricing policies, the same sales strategy that produced good results elsewhere didn't register in Amarillo.

So Bud Phillips headed out to the Panhandle of Texas and began interviewing Amarillo housewives and grocery shoppers of both sexes and all ages. His research uncovered two problem areas for the client.

First, because Borden's plant sat near the train depot in Amarillo, many people assumed Borden shipped in its milk from out of state. That assumption about the milk's freshness raised some concern about spoilage. Second, the roads leading into the plant were unpaved and filled with potholes. Dust, dirt and grime clung to the Borden delivery trucks that rumbled in and out of the plant all day. Phillips found that many shoppers thought dirty trucks meant dirty milk.

Armed with these facts, Morris Hite devised a local newspaper campaign that addressed the twin problems of freshness and spoilage. Full-page ads in the Amarillo *Globe News* carried pictures of local dairy farmers and identified them as the suppliers of Borden's milk. "I PRODUCE AMARILLO'S BEST TASTIN' MILK," proclaimed the headlines over the ads, while the body copy gave a biographical sketch of the dairymen.

Borden's local plant manager, working with city officials, had the roads leading into the plant paved, eliminating much of the image problem. The company invested money to improve the overall appearance of the milk plant and began washing each milk truck daily as part of its fleet maintenance. Complaints about dirty trucks disappeared.

In sum, shortly after Bud Phillips' research had isolated the problems in Amarillo, the plant began producing sales results in line with company expectations.

Tracy-Locke's digging for facts also solved a problem for Chance-Vought (the forerunner to LTV Corp.), which had experienced poor results with its recruitment advertising. The company had been trying a traditional approach, buying large-space newspaper ads that said "We need so many engineers for this function, so many engineers for that function,"—publishing the cumulative number of employees the growing defense contractor needed to recruit.

Tracy-Locke intervened with a better idea. Jack Taylor and Bud Phillips conducted in-depth interviews with graduate students in engineering at leading U.S. colleges and universities and learned that engineers prize their individuality. They did not wish to be pegged as members of some group. They wanted to be seen as individuals. Period.

So Tracy-Locke went to Chance-Vought's advertising manager, Johnny Johnson, and sold him on the merits of a recruitment campaign that focused on individual Chance-Vought employees. The ads showed a picture of a successful young engineer and said "We're looking for an engineer like John Doe." The body copy told a story about how Mr. Doe worked in an exciting area of development, how he handled responsibility, how he had a great sense of accomplishment with his job.

The message rang true with prospective engineers. They could see themselves following in John Doe's footsteps. A challenging, rewarding career at Chance-Vought sounded like something seriously to consider. As a result, the client suddenly found itself flooded with applications from top students at top schools. The campaign reduced Chance-Vought's recruiting costs and upgraded its employee base.

Research helped Tracy-Locke sell another important piece of business, First National Bank in Dallas. The agency conducted an independent research campaign that showed a serious disparity between the bank's advertising slogan "Give Us An Opportunity To Say Yes" and its lending policies. Dallas businessmen desperately seeking capital and credit lines knew not to count on First National.

Explained Morris Hite: "We went out and talked to about 35 business people in Dallas, people with major businesses around town, and we found out the bank had a terrible reputation. The loan officers weren't eager to help business grow."

The Tracy-Locke account men heard horror stories. Said Hite: "For example, in the case of Luby's Cafeterias, Luby's had come to them wanting to borrow money and the banker asked them why and Luby's said it wanted to

Young Morris Hite.

A big wheel in Anadarko.

The budding artist/copywriter.

The Tracy-Locke-Dawson staff (circa 1930) assembled on the top of the Majestic Theater building in downtown Dallas.

Morris Hite with Don Luce on LT352.

WWII buddies: Tom Yost, Don Luce, Morris Hite.

A brief fling at flight instruction.

Tracy-Locke founder Ray Locke (center) with staff in 1948. From left: Ernest Lovan, Scott Leonard, (Locke), Morris Hite, Stanley Foran.

Hite takes charge in March 1950.

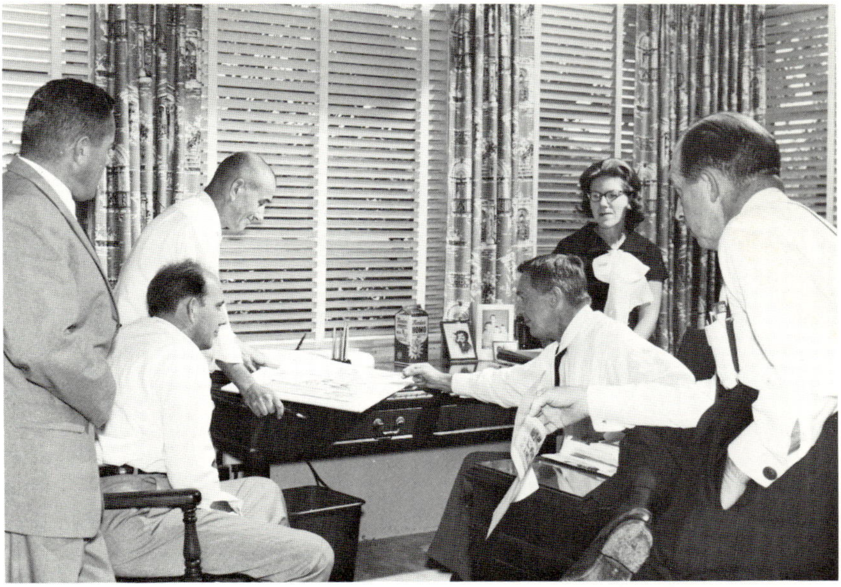

Hite and staff discuss Borden's creative. From left: Bill James, Bud Phillips (seated), Iggy Sahula-Dycke, Morris Hite, Luellyn Wright, Larry DuPont.

Morris Hite (l.) and Bud Phillips (r.) flank chart showing "How Much, How Good" survey for Imperial Sugar.

Hite and Imperial Sugar president Bob Armstrong review "Teena's Cookbook" campaign.

Hite at Tracy-Locke's 50th anniversary party in 1963 with Glenn Addington (c.) and Joe Dawson.

The board of directors of Tracy-Locke Co. Front row: Bud Phillips, Morris Hite, Norm Campbell, Bill Neale. Back row: Tom Forman, Jack Taylor, Stewart Mitchell, Bob Brown.

Morris Hite chosen 1967 "Man of the Year" by the North Texas Chapter of the American Marketing Association.

Hite receives the 1969 Linz Award for public service in Dallas from Albert Hirsch (c.) and Jim Chambers (r.).

At the reception for the Horatio Alger Award. From left: Stewart Mitchell, Caroline Hite, Morris Hite, Judi Hancock, Norm Campbell.

Morris Hite celebrates 65th birthday with protegés Norm Campbell (l.) and Bob Brown.

The Hite kids:
front: Florence, Aimee
back: Jerry, Sissy, Lee.

The last photo taken of Caroline and Morris Hite together.

expand to Denver. And First National's loan officer said to the Luby's people, 'Why would you want to go and do a thing like that?' You shouldn't take that kind of risk. You've got things going good for you just as they are.' The bank turned down the request."

"Anyway, our research study showed First National had a reputation as a moss-backed bank. I took the study, a damning study, down to show Bob Stewart who had just taken over at First National. I figured he'd either throw me out of his office or he'd listen and get some guidance on what he needed to do to revitalize his business.

"We didn't have his account, so it wasn't like we were taking any chance. I said 'You talk about being a Yes bank but in reality you're perceived as a No bank.' He listened attentively, and after I'd given my whole speech he said to me, 'Do you mind doing that again?'"

Stewart called in his top executives and Hite repeated his presentation for them. Then Stewart spoke. "This is exactly what I've been trying to tell you," he chided. "That we've got to get off our duff, we've got to be aggressive, we've got to correct this image."

So Stewart saw to it that First National Bank began saying yes to creditworthy customers. "Yes" was also Stewart's reply when Morris Hite asked if Tracy-Locke could take over the bank's ad budget.

In the mid-1950s, Tracy-Locke devised its own measure of advertising effectiveness, called the "How Much, How Good" test. Based on the Ted Bates agency's "usage-pull" test, Tracy-Locke's measured whether ad messages were absorbed and retained.

Explained Hite: "This was a tremendous selling device for us. We were the only people in the area who had anything like it. We'd go out and ask people, 'What brand of bread did you buy last?' Then we'd ask them 'Have you seen or heard any Mrs Baird's advertising recently?' If the answer was 'No,' the interview was over. But if the answer was 'Yes,' they had seen the advertising, then we'd ask 'What did the advertising say?'

"If they could tell us the ad message, then we knew that person had really heard or seen the ad. We could correlate that number of people who knew the advertising to the brand purchased last."

In the case of Regal Beer, Tracy-Locke's "How Much, How Good" research revealed that people who knew about the beer bought it less than the people who didn't know a thing about it. Not a comforting proposition for any marketer.

Said Hite: "Our research revealed that the 'Swing To Regal' campaign scored exceptional penetration. More than 50 percent of the beer drinkers in New Orleans could recall the sense of the message without prompting. That was the good news. The bad news was that Regal had only about a third as many buyers among those who were aware of the advertising. There was absolutely no evidence of the advertising's causing anybody to swing to Regal. Actually, the advertising was driving drinkers away from the brand.

"Beer drinkers are no different from other consumers. They don't like to be misled or taken for chumps. They knew there was no swing to Regal. When they went into taverns, they saw everybody drinking Falstaff or Jax. The campaign was a hoax. The people at Regal were trying to kid them and subconsciously they resented it.

"Actually, the campaign was causing people to take more than normal notice of what brand their neighbors were drinking. Inadvertently, Regal was accelerating the swing away from its own brand. One of the most powerful of advertising forces is the unspoken endorsement a brand gets when it is seen to be chosen by large numbers of satisfied customers. Regal Beer was putting that force to work for its competition."

Tracy-Locke's research also addressed the issue of

Regal Beer's quality. "We wanted to assure ourselves that any quality problems with the brand in the past had been corrected," said Hite. "Contrary to what self-appointed protectors of the consumer so loudly proclaim, advertising does not cause people to buy bad products. Nothing will put a bad product out of business faster than a good advertising campaign.

"Advertising causes people to try a product once, but poor quality eliminates any possibility of a repeat purchase. Furthermore, disappointed one-time buyers will tell their friends. No product can make it with one-time buyers. Neither can any product survive the unfavorable word-of-mouth advertising created by poor quality."

Research showed that Regal's quality problems had been alleviated. Tracy-Locke conducted its own taste tests with consumers that showed Regal could more than hold its own with other brands in the market. In fact, Tracy-Locke based a creative campaign for Regal (after the threatened union boycott had been called off) on a series of comparative taste tests.

"We created radio commercials and newspaper ads that said 'In side-by-side taste tests 136 out of 189 people chose Regal over the brand they had been drinking.' The next week, the numbers would be 242 out of 335 people chose Regal, and so on."

The ad campaign brought a complaint from a competitor which petitioned the Federal Alcohol and Tobacco Tax Commission to halt Regal's ad practices. "The Commission like all government bodies, always knows what is best for you and me," observed Hite. "They must protect us from our own folly. They ruled taste is too subjective a sensation to be measured accurately in simple side-by-side tests. After all, what would a bunch of dumb Louisiana beer drinkers know about taste?"

The campaign ran for nearly 60 days and helped Regal regain some market share. Interestingly enough, two decades later Pepsi-Cola based its advertising strategy on side-by-side taste tests with Coca-Cola. The Pepsi Challenge captured national attention; the Regal Challenge did not.

Perhaps no single incident validated Tracy-Locke's use and understanding of research more than its winning approval from Anheuser-Busch to handle a major push in Texas for the Budweiser brand.

Hite and Phillips had conducted extensive research on beer consumption patterns in the southern states. Not only for Regal Beer, but for Carta Blanca and Pearl Brewing Co., two companies with which it had discussed doing business on and off.

When Anheuser-Busch announced its plans to promote Budweiser heavily in Texas, it began looking for a Texas shop to coordinate the campaign. The name Tracy-Locke, the Dallas agency with the grocery store expertise, kept popping up.

To win the assignment, Morris Hite had to give a market analysis and marketing strategy to Anheuser-Busch officials. He traveled to St. Louis, accompanied by Clay Stephenson, to make his report.

The Dallas admen were ushered into a conference room and told to set up their flip chart presentation at the end of a long conference table. At the other end of the table appeared to be a throne. The room filled up with Anheuser-Busch marketing executives but no one said a word. Presently, in walked August A. Busch, Jr.

"Okay Mr. Hite," Busch said. "You're going to tell us about selling beer in Texas. Please begin."

Hite began his presentation. He'd prepared 75 flip charts, enough to make the Anheuser-Busch people's eyes bug out like shrimp. He tapped his foot uncontrollably as he spoke about Budweiser having low brand awareness among Texas consumers. It finished behind Falstaff, Pearl,

Grand Prize and other labels in name recognition. When consumers were asked about Bud specifically, they rated it exceptionally high in taste and overall quality.

Not more than 10 minutes into his presentation the old man cut Morris off.

"Sit down, Mr. Hite," motioned August Busch. Hite sat down, wondering how he'd blown his big chance.

"Gentlemen," said August Busch, eyeing his staff, "our friend Mr. Hite has told me more about beer in the past few minutes than all of you have told me the past few months. Hire him."

With that, Busch smiled at Morris Hite and walked out of the room.

Hite could scarcely believe what he'd just witnessed. He'd barely begun his pitch. He got back up and walked over to the flip chart. "Does anyone want to see the rest of my presentation?" Morris said to no one in particular.

"We just bought it," came the reply. "We might as well see it."

CHAPTER ELEVEN

"WHAT THE HELL DO YOU WRITERS DO? I WALK THROUGH THE CREATIVE DEPARTMENT AT LEAST THREE TIMES A DAY AND I HARDLY EVER HEAR A TYPEWRITER GOING."—MORRIS HITE

Tracy-Locke once again relied on research to land San Antonio-based Pearl Brewing Co. in 1960. A popular regional brand with a sizable advertising budget, Pearl lifted Tracy-Locke's billings to roughly $10 million. "It took us to a new plateau," observed Hite.

Tracy-Locke pitched for Pearl's account in a spirited competition against three other agencies including the incumbent, The Pitluk Group in San Antonio. Clay Stephenson & Associates in Houston also competed, and Stephenson's presence posed a special challenge to Hite. He damn sure didn't care to lose to the man whose business methods he'd criticized during their split the year before.

Hite believed from the outset that Tracy-Locke should center its pitch to Pearl around water. Other regional brewers, Hamms in the Midwest and Olympia in the far Northwest, had scored success by intimating that water played a more pivotal part in the brewing process than barley, oats, hops or any of the other ingredients found in beer. Morris believed the same strategy could be adapted to Pearl.

Pearl had been using the ad slogan "Brewed With Pure Artesian Spring Water," but Morris considered the reference too general and imprecise. He felt a claim about the water used in brewing Pearl beer should be more specific and direct.

"Hell, artesian water sometimes is bad water," he pointed out. "All artesian water means is water that comes up from the ground under its own force. Gases down in the earth have a lifting power that brings artesian water to the surface."

Hite dispatched his research men and account men to find out more about the water used in brewing Pearl beer. They tapped into information stored at the Texas Water Resources Board and hit a wellspring.

Noted Hite: "We learned that a wonderful stream of water flowed under San Antonio. It was formed up on the Edwards Plateau area of Texas, one of the greatest natural spring regions in the whole United States. During the rainy season, water comes from natural springs and filters underground through the porous riverbeds of limestone rock and into an underground stream known as the Edwards Aquifer.

"The stream flows underneath the city of San Antonio and is tapped a quarter to a half-mile under the ground. This artesian well is used in the brewing of Pearl Beer and makes it one of the finest brewing waters in the world."

Tracy-Locke had found its hook. The agency also learned that an estimated 1,000 to 1,200 natural springs fed the Edwards Aquifer. The information provided the agency with its *big idea*. Pearl Beer would become known for being brewed with water from "The Country of 1,100 Springs."

Broadcast producers Larry DuPont and Howard Fisher began scouting locations on the Edwards Plateau, a region Morris Hite and others at the agency knew from deer hunting trips. Don Young, one of the artists, drew a stunning series of pastel renderings of the Edwards Plateau for magazine and newspaper ads and point-of-sale materials. Bill Mitchell and Alan Meyer started cranking out the copy.

"We romanced the way the water came to San Antonio. We used beautiful pictures of the Hill Country of

Texas, one of the most beautiful parts of the whole United States, to make the point," said Hite.

To win Pearl beer, Hite had to convince members of the Koehler family, which owned the brewery, that he would personally be involved with the account. Rival agencies frequently pitched against Tracy-Locke by saying "Morris Hite will come in and charm your socks off, but after you sign on with Tracy-Locke you'll hardly ever see him again. He's spread too thin. You think you're getting him for your account, but you're really not."

Hite assured Pearl's management he'd keep close tabs on the account. And as a sign of how much he valued the account, he promised to dispatch Bill James, the agency's executive vice president, to head the San Antonio office. James later lured Bob Brown away from Clay Stephenson to serve as account supervisor on Pearl.

The Pearl campaign reflected Morris's view on advertising creativity: once you find the big idea—in Pearl's case the "Country of 1,100 Springs"—you've completed the difficult part. Creative execution should not be too difficult to achieve if the idea is sound and on target. As Hite observed: "If you have a great idea, your secretary can write the copy."

When Morris locked in on what he considered the correct selling message, he seldom departed from it. His approach to creativity could safely be called conservative. Tracy-Locke didn't take unnecessary chances, didn't break much new ground. Its creative attitude embodied the Texas expression *if it ain't broke, don't fix it.*

For example, Tracy-Locke research in the mid-1950s for Mrs Baird's Bread revealed that shoppers familiar with the story of the family enterprise bought more bread than those who were not. That suggested to Hite that the TV commercials should highlight the family story.

Larry DuPont and the creatives developed a TV commercial in which a grandmother gives her granddaughter an account of how Mrs. Ninnie L. Baird baked fresh bread each morning and how her sons made household deliveries on bicycles.

The TV commercial scored exceedingly high scores on the "How Much, How Good" test and helped Mrs Baird's Bread take away market share from its competitors. The Baird family story remained the centerpiece of the company's advertising thereafter.

Though Baird family members showed initial reluctance to appear in the commercials themselves, they couldn't argue with the impact the spots had on sales. As the years rolled by, Tracy-Locke's TV commercials trumpeted how a Baird family member personally supervised the baking, just as Ninnie Baird had done generations before.

The acquisition of the Pearl account lifted Tracy-Locke to a new level of prosperity and as a sign of its success, the agency moved into a new headquarters building near Central Expressway and Haskell. Dubbed the "House That Morris Built," the office opening served as a significant milestone in Tracy-Locke's golden anniversary year.

Working with Clutts and Parker (architects), Mayes and Brockette (structural engineers) and Gregerson and Gaynor (mechanical engineers), Hite took pains to arrange the agency's offices in a manner that would expedite the business. Included in the 36,000 sq. ft. of working space was a test kitchen where Luellyn Wright, the copywriter/home economist, could test new recipes for her Imperial Sugar Co. cookbooks or new dips to eat with Fritos. Morris, who liked to pass through the test kitchen and nibble, dreamed up some of the recipes himself.

The building seemed to have everything an ad agency would need, except for enough parking spaces for the 86 members of the Dallas staff. For all his calculations about the traffic flow within an agency, Hite had neglected to consider the traffic arriving at the agency. Tracy-Locke leased temporary parking spaces for some staffers, but the situation seemed unsatisfactory. The agency toyed with the idea of building a parking garage next to the building but later dropped the plans.

Just before the grand opening of Tracy-Locke's new home, Morris received a letter from Joe Dawson, which read: "As the last remaining member of the original three, it gives me great pleasure to realize the excellent job you and your associates have done, culminating in the move to your own building.

"I am indeed proud of you and am confident that this is just another step to future progress."

Tracy-Locke's new building offered visible evidence of the agency's success to the Dallas business community. Another sign could be seen in the account men representing the agency in the mid-1960s.

Rough-hewn Morris Hite had surrounded himself with what folks back in Anadarko might have called city slickers. Fred Rowe, the executive vice president, was an Ivy League man from Princeton. Stewart Mitchell, one of the rising stars in account service, had worked in New York and had a Madison Avenue veneer. So did Paul Rafferty, Gene Thomas, Jack Jordan and Norm Campbell.

The Tracy-Locke account men embodied their counterparts on Madison Avenue. They took themselves, and their accounts, seriously. They were hard-working and hyper. Hite gave them room to operate and they did.

Tracy-Locke had little of the hijinks and tomfoolery typically associated with many ad agencies, and few of the zany characters. About as much color as you could find at Tracy-Locke was at the drawing board of artist Iggy Sahula-Dycke, who always wore a hat while he worked.

The agency engaged in advertising, not antics. Even the creative guys like Bill Neale and Larry DuPont wore white shirts and ties. If you wanted fun and games look somewhere else; fun to Tracy-Locke meant making money.

Hite repeated his Account Executive's Training School in the early 1960s, mainly because of the new faces swelling the account service ranks. His motivation this time had nothing to do with lackadaisical performance. To the contrary, he could see a sense of urgency everywhere he looked. He merely wanted the younger account men like Willard Moon, Carl Larkin, Dick Craiglow and Marshall Bateman to receive exposure to his thinking.

Morris realized his own role within the agency had changed. He still kept current on all the accounts by wading through conference reports, still had a major voice in creative directions, still edited every marketing plan. Yet he needed to allot fewer and fewer hours to servicing accounts. His account men had things under control.

Hite could see what Tracy-Locke's maturation meant to the agency. It coincided with the beginning of mass marketing in the U.S., a phenomenon primarily ushered in by television. American families were bigger and more affluent, and the way to their hearts and minds—and wallets and purses—was through television. Agencies with a track record in broadcast advertising were about to catch a big wave.

Tracy-Locke added a second major creative triumph to its Pearl success with its rollout of a new Frito-Lay chip, Doritos, in 1966.

The agency had been working with the Frito-Lay account since the mid-1950s. While the Lay's potato chip brand had been assigned to a New York agency, Tracy-Locke had picked up the company's first product, the Frito corn chip, in 1954.

A dozen years later it received the assignment to introduce a new chip, called Doritos, which Frito-Lay officials envisioned primarily as a regional brand. It knew it could sell the chip in the Southwest where Mexican foods and Mexican-type products had strong appeal.

But Tracy-Locke demonstrated through its sales promotion and in-store merchandising that Doritos had a broader sales potential than the Southwest. Based on its success in test markets and its first phase of distribution, Frito-Lay increased the number of markets in which Doritos were sold. The brand more than held its own wherever it went.

Again, timing had been critical. Doritos arrived just as America's first generation of junk food junkies came to the fore. With its clout in snack food category already established, Frito-Lay could get the shelf-space for the new brand. Junksters knew the Frito-Lay name and seemed ready for a line extension.

The Tracy-Locke team of Jim Albright and Ron McQuien would build the agency's creative strategy effort around the concept of freshness, and agency copywriter Jack Ciaccio penned a memorable line: "Taste As Good As They Crunch." Creatives and account service people jousted over whether the line should be "They Taste As Good As They Crunch" with creatives winning the verdict.

The award-winning TV campaign that supported the national rollout of Doritos featured Canadian actor Avery Schreiber. Scenarios called for Schreiber to perform a variety of tasks only to be disrupted by the noise of some bystander biting into a Doritos chip. The signature of the spots had Schreiber doing a slow-burn into the camera and then exacting his "revenge" by biting into a Doritos of his own.

"This campaign was born in extreme pain," said Hite. "After many hours of searching, the creative group decided that the one most distinctive feature of Doritos was its crunchiness. Unquestionably it is the most crunchy of all snack products. So we had the *crunchiest* product on the market. We had served Doritos for several years and written many TV spots and the idea had been there all the time. Nobody had isolated crunchiness as a unique point of difference.

"There it was. The big idea. All it needed was an eye-popping and believable presentation. The creative group came up with a powerful execution. Probably the most outstanding spot of the series shows Avery Schreiber as the pool hustler who rips the pool table cloth as his concentration is disrupted. The spot has everything—the big idea, high interest and entertainment value, humor and strong product identity."

The TV commercials attracted a strong following, sales shot upward, and over time, Doritos replaced Fritos as the company's best-selling snack chip.

The Doritos story represented a milestone for Tracy-Locke, its first national success. More important, it demonstrated the agency's marketing savvy with Frito-Lay's parent company, Pepsico. By the 1980s, Pepsico had grown into a billion-dollar food and beverage behemoth with a nine-figure ad budget. Those were the kinds of friends an ad agency likes to have.

Advertising agencies can be characterized as either account service-driven or creative-driven. A rare few shops manage to strike a delicate balance between the two disciplines, but most tend to tilt one way or the other. Heavily.

That fact of ad agency life stems from observable differences between account service people and creative people. Account service people thrive on order and organization, planning, analysis, and step-by-step rational judgment; creative people thrive on spontaneity, inspiration, whims, flights of fantasy and seat-of-the-pants emotional calls.

Account service people have one set of personality traits, creative people another. Account service people are left-brain dominant, creative people right-brain dominant. Account service people tend to vote Republican; creative people tend to vote Democrat, if at all. Account service people are Felix Ungers; creative people are Oscar Madisons.

If account people pronounced the word tomato TOE-MAY-TOE, creative people would make a point of saying TOE-MAH-TOE. Given such irreconcilable differences, the two disciplines engage in a constant battle for power and control. Fighting is as instinctive as that between cats and dogs.

An agency's position on the account service/creative scale comes from the top. It flows downhill, not uphill. Given Hite's belief that account executives are the key players at an agency, guess which way Tracy-Locke leaned? Creatives took a back seat at the shop. They didn't lack talent, only clout.

Examples? In the mid-1960s, Tracy-Locke had no creative director, nominally one of the most powerful positions in the ad agency structure. The agency had a vice president/copy, Bill Mitchell, and a vice president/art chief, Bill Neale, and vice president/broadcast services, Larry DuPont.

But it had no creative director. No one person with overall responsibility for the agency's creative output. At least not officially. The agency's creative director, *de facto*, was Morris Hite.

Regardless of the creative structure, the agency managed to turn out some memorable advertising. Beginning in the early 1950s, Hite showed an affinity for a 10-second spot by creating a cartoon character called "Impy" for Imperial Sugar Co. Impy sprang to life off the Imperial label and dived into a glass of liquid with a high-pitched yelp, "It's Quick-Dissolvin'".

Other sugars dissolved quickly, too, but Morris' line served as a preemptive claim. The voice, patterned after actor Andy Devine, added a recognition factor to the Imperial Sugar spot.

Hite also used animation effectively in a TV campaign for Haggar Apparel Co. The spot, called "Dancin' Slacks," borrowed from the dancing cigarette spot Old Gold cigarettes had made several years before. The ad pulled attention toward the Haggar line.

By the time Tracy-Locke scored its major creative successes for Pearl and Frito-Lay, advertising's creative revolution of the 1960s was in full flower. No one figure epitomized the creative revolution more than Bill Bernbach of Doyle Dane Bernbach. Bernbach's shop created for Volkswagen such incandescent ad lines as "Lemon" and "Think Small"—which not only attracted a generation of car buyers to Volkswagen and brought cult status to the VW Beetle, but changed the whole perspective of American car buyers.

Americans began thinking real small, all right, after the Arab oil embargo of the early 1970s shot gasoline prices to $1.50 a gallon and created shortages at the pump. Small suddenly seemed better than large. Infinitely better.

In 1967, Morris Hite served as the secretary-treasurer of the American Association of Advertising Agencies—or as it's called in the trade, the 4A's. The group consists of most of the industry's larger shops. Tracy-Locke-Dawson had become a member years earlier. That same year, one of the directors of the 4A's was none other than Bill Bernbach.

The exposure to advertising's acknowledged top creative mind produced some changes in Hite. Bernbach had pioneered the concept of the creative team, where an art director and writer worked in tandem. The most famous team, writer Julian Koenig and art director Helmut Krone, collaborated with Bernbach on the Volkswagen ads. Tracy-Locke began experimenting with creative teams, not wholesale but by degrees.

By the late 1960s, the creative department at Tracy-

Locke mirrored the changes in the times. The creative staff, the younger ones anyway, started sporting long hair, beards and moustaches, guerrilla-type clothes. One creative copywriter, Jim Albright, gained notoriety within the agency for his motorcycle helmet, field artillery coat and motorcycle boots. He dressed straight out of the Hell's Angels handbook.

Though several account people groused about such expressions of individuality, Hite took it all in stride. As he said about one flamboyantly dressed copywriter: "I don't care if he has an American flag tattooed to his ass and comes to work naked—if he can write."

What Morris couldn't take in stride, though, was the upheaval in the creative ranks generated when Hite hired the first high-ticket, bonafide creative director, Kevin Begos.

Begos represented a strong personality and the ego and temperament of an artist. He could be brusque, short and cutting with employees. Coming from Madison Avenue (Dancer Fitzgerald Sample) where creatives wielded the power, Begos was used to getting his way.

His arrival triggered the departure of several creatives, including longtime hands. Hite hated to see the loss of these people, but felt he had to give Begos room to operate.

But as the months went by a rift developed between account service and creative. In one memorable shouting match, mild-mannered Fred Rowe leapt out of his seat and nearly came to blows with Begos. The episode showed how tense things had become.

Finally, Hite could no longer ignore the commotion. Morris cut the cord on his first high-powered creative director. If this were the price to be paid for creativity, forget it. The price came too high.

The 1960s ended with account service maintaining the power at Tracy-Locke, as had been true of the other six decades in the agency's past.

CHAPTER TWELVE

"IN DALLAS, IT'S NOT HOW LONG YOU'VE BEEN HERE, IT'S NOT WHO YOU KNOW, IT'S WHAT YOU CAN DO THAT COUNTS."—MORRIS HITE

Tracy-Locke's sustained growth in the 1960s, in no small part based on its success with Pearl and Frito-Lay, gave Morris Hite freedom to expand his activities beyond advertising. Seeing a new level of proficiency in the agency's account service, Hite eased back on his own involvement with the day-to-day operations. He still made all the big decisions at Tracy-Locke, but fewer of the little ones. He mastered the possibilities of delegation.

By the mid-1960s, Morris began devoting increasing amounts of time to civic pursuits. By the late-1960s, he worked as much on the city of Dallas's business as on Tracy-Locke's; he became the agency's chief executive officer *in absentia*.

"Run By Businessmen for Businessmen" might be an unofficial motto for Dallas. The heads of the downtown banks, insurance companies, law firms and real estate companies have always exercised an active hand in guiding the city's development. That was certainly so in the 1960s, when the slate for the mayor's office and city council posts rested in the hands of the Dallas Citizens Council. The DCC, a group of roughly 200 power brokers, ran Dallas with an iron-fistedness and machine-like efficiency that Richard Daley would have admired.

As the head of the city's largest and most prosperous advertising agency, Morris didn't hesitate to accept the DCC's invitation for him to join their group. He prized his new affiliation both personally and professionally. He began accepting assignments—a United Fund drive here, a Red Cross drive there, the Better Business Bureau board—because the Dallas way of doing *bidness* demands that corporate executives make civic contributions. It's a rite of passage into the ring of power.

"Ours is a business-oriented society. The business community, not the political body, is what *makes* a city," observed Hite, reflecting the majority view in Dallas. "If a city fails to grow, the business community is to blame. Not the politicians. Because if the political body is bad, the business community *should replace it*."

The business community had its work cut out after the assassination of President John F. Kennedy. Following the tragedy of November 22, 1963, the national press corps inspected the city and found it repressed and oppressive, backward and bigoted, and populated with political extremists and kooks. And those were some of its better points.

The stigma of small-mindedness stuck throughout much of the 1960s. TV commentator Eric Sevaried coined a phrase for Dallas—the "City of Hate"—and described Dallas as being at an awkward stage of adolescence. "It grew up too quickly," he said. "It is a metropolis in body but not yet in spirit."

Within the city limits, however, Dallas began to expand its vision and shape its own destiny. Mayor J. Erik Jonsson in December 1965 met with 26 community leaders and established a program called "Goals for Dallas." The program addressed urban issues such as government and city services, transportation, education, health, welfare, arts and entertainment and drew participation for all segments of the city—rich and poor, black, white and Hispanic.

Jonsson, one of the driving forces behind Texas Instruments, brought the business discipline of long-term strategic planning to the city. His Goals for Dallas program would directly involve over 100,000 Dallas citizens in the process of ranking the city's needs and planning schedules and systems to accomplish the goals.

In 1967, Dallas took a dramatic step toward the future by proposing a $175 million bond package to voters that included funding for a new convention center and city hall, as well as earmarking funds for Dallas' part of a new Dallas/Fort Worth regional airport.

Mayor Jonsson tapped Dallas businessman Joe Haggar, the younger of the two Haggar brothers working at Haggar Co., to spearhead support for the capital improvements package. The campaign promised anything but slack time for the slacks manufacturer, since as Haggar recalled, "It was the largest bond election we'd ever undertaken in the history of Dallas. We had 14 propositions on the ballot. And some formidable opposition for each one."

The two most critical propositions on the ballot addressed enlarging and modernizing the Dallas Memorial Auditorium and convention center, and approving the regional airport. Dallas had ranked as high as third in convention trade in the United States, but had slipped to fifth in 1966. Even that level of business seemed surprising for a city that offered none of the bright lights and after-hours entertainment of a Las Vegas, New York, or Miami.

The implications for the airport would be even more far-reaching for an inland city like Dallas. Supporters like R.L. Thornton, Jr. said "Air is our ocean and the airport will be our port." Other propositions to be decided included funds for a new city hall and a renovation to the State Fair.

Staffers at city hall had prepared materials to use in a public information effort to build support for the bond campaign, but Joe Haggar found them to be mechanical and ponderous. Long on statistics, short on salesmanship, in other words.

Haggar knew that to spur support and overcome voter apathy, the bond proposal needed a dramatic focus, a call to action. So Haggar turned to the best communicator he knew, the man who'd been responsible for calling attention to Haggar slacks for the past 27 years—Morris Hite.

Tracy-Locke conducted independent research to isolate the major voter concerns, then Morris and his staff boiled down the "reason-why" to support the $175 million package into a simple, memorable phrase. They called it "Crossroads."

Dallas voters faced a crossroads, the agency insisted, and they could move forward by voting for the 13 propositions or move backward by voting them down. To illustrate the point, Tracy-Locke used TV, radio, newspapers and outdoor advertising to tell the story of how Jefferson, Texas, once faced a similar crossroads.

Financial baron Jay Gould and representatives of western railroad interests came to Texas in 1870 and announced plans to make Jefferson the distribution center of the Southwest. But the people of Jefferson spurned the railroads' interests, jacking up the price on land the railroad men wished to acquire. As Morris Hite put it, "[The people of Jefferson] could not see the future for the obstructing view of the fast buck."

Not disposed to stay where he wasn't welcome, Jay Gould left town. He wrote in the Excelsior Hotel's register the fateful words, "The end of Jefferson, Texas." Gould fired this parting shot at the citizenry: *"Grass will grow in your streets."* Not that he was bitter or anything.

In 1872, Dallas ensured its future by catering to the railroad interests. The 227 qualified voters in Dallas passed a $100 thousand bond issue to finance railroad facilities and provide the railroads with free land.

"It was a gigantic undertaking for Dallas. The citizens were far less able to support a $100 thousand bond issue then than we are to support $175 million today. And the supporters had some opposition. But the people with foresight won the day and Dallas was on its way to greatness."

So said Morris Hite at numerous speeches he made to civic, professional and social organizations in the city. "Our speakers bureau on the Crossroads campaign reached 50,000 people and I must have talked to 4,000 myself," Hite recalled.

Dallas developed as the distribution center of the Southwest in the late 19th and early 20th century. It subsequently grew to be the nation's largest inland city without water transportation, overcoming such a distinct handicap through a transportation network of rails and highways.

By 1967, Jefferson sat tucked away in northeast Texas near the Louisiana border, a sleepy little town of 2,900 people. Dallas had nearly a million people in its metropolitan area, the State Fair of Texas, Neiman-Marcus and Tom Landry and the Dallas Cowboys. It had become "Big D."

"We reminded the citizens of Dallas what happened in Jefferson," Hite explained. "We reminded them that Jefferson had failed to make the right decision at the crossroads and that Dallas was faced with a crossroads in 1967. We told the people of Dallas if you want to get away from traffic problems, taxes and all the frustrations of living in a dynamic city, you might consider moving to Jefferson. You might not be able to make a living there, but your taxes should be lower."

On the eve of the election, Tracy-Locke placed double-truck ads and special sections in the Dallas newspapers. The Dallas voters got the message. On Aug. 8, 1963, the voters opted overwhelmingly for growth, passing all 14 issues by margins of 2-to-1 or greater. The city's leaders had ensured that Dallas would move forward in dramatic fashion.

"I don't think we've ever seen so many people from so many parts of town with so many different political views work together so closely or so well," said Joe Haggar, quick to credit Tracy-Locke for its galvanizing role in the bond election.

In 1968, Morris Hite took over as president of the Dallas Chamber of Commerce. The post, in addition to its business development responsibilities, gave Hite ambassadorial duties at a host of city functions. Morris made welcoming remarks at the convention center, took part in ground-breakings, ribbon-cuttings and topping-out ceremonies, and generally enjoyed all aspects of the Chamber job, except perhaps the interminable cocktail receptions.

Hite possessed a flair for public speaking, enhanced by all the years of flip-chart presentations to agency clients and prospects. He also welcomed the chance to brag about Big D. When he wasn't putting Dallas on a pedestal, though, he was putting himself down with a self-deprecating wit. At many Chamber-related functions, Morris told about receiving a letter that started out:

"Dear Mr. Hite: "With a fathead like you running the Dallas Chamber of Commerce, it's no wonder Houston is growing so fast . . ."

Morris also liked to tell a story on himself about how shortly after World War II he had conducted a market survey for a Mexican brewery, Cerveceria Cuauhtemoc, based in Monterrey. The brewery wanted to distribute Carta Blanca beer in Texas and asked Tracy-Locke to help with a market analysis and distribution plan. Morris made the agency's presentation to brewery officials through an interpreter, a laborious process. Months later, after the project had been scrapped, he learned that the president of Cerveceria Cuauhtemoc had been educated at Massachusetts Institute of Technology. "He could speak better English than anyone present, including the guy who made the presentation," laughed Morris.

Hite never seemed at a loss for good things to say about Dallas. It went with the job, of course. As he told a convention of high school students: "Dallas is a young man's city. Some of the city's outstanding business successes have been achieved by very young men. In Dallas, it's not how long you've been here—it's not who you know—it's what you can do that counts."

Or a meeting of city planners: "A city is like a business. A business may be equipped with the most advanced and highly automated equipment known to science. But if it is not staffed with energetic, hard-working people and courageous, farsighted leaders, it will not prosper. Likewise, a city's present and future depends upon its people. Not just its leaders. Good leadership is required, but the attitude of the smallest homeowner, the feelings of the man in the street have a bearing upon a city's present and future."

Or a meeting of national black leaders: "I am greatly pleased to welcome the Urban League to Dallas. We at the Chamber of Commerce welcome the opportunity of working with you to help create new employment and career opportunities for Negro people in Dallas. We at the Chamber believe that the answer to most of the problems of all unfortunate people, black or white, can be solved by education, employment and enterprise.

Selling the attributes of Dallas came as naturally to Hite as selling the attributes of Borden milk. As Hite explained to a gathering of American Marketing Association executives in May 1968:

"Every business, every service, every situation responds to good marketing principles. Four of the fundamentals of marketing success are:

1. Improve the product
2. Make the product more available
3. Make the price more competitive
4. Present product advantages in terms of user benefits."

Hite outlined for the marketers how the leadership of Dallas applied those principles to the city's most pressing problems, which included upgrading educational opportunities, improving transportation, continuing to attract new business and industry, and continuing to improve relations.

"Let's take educational capabilities," said Hite. "Educated manpower is part of our product. We must produce more educated manpower if Dallas is going to continue to grow. That's principle one. We must make higher education more readily available and at a competitive cost. That's two and three. We must develop a plan that the entire community will back and sell it. That's principle four."

One of the highlights of Hite's two years as president of the Dallas Chamber of Commerce came when he took the lead in establishing a program called Job Fair, which helped minority and disadvantaged youth aged 16 to 22 find summer jobs. "Poor kids have not had the opportunity to earn before," said Hite. "Most of them are anxious to work. I know that the employment of these youngsters will be of great benefit to Dallas," beamed Hite. "Substantial wages will be paid and hopefully, many of these boys and girls will be able to save enough money to help them continue their schooling."

Hite knew, of course, that high levels of youth unemployment in metropolitan areas like Los Angeles and Detroit had contributed to the riots and demonstrations during the "long hot summers" of the mid-1960s. He wanted to defuse the likelihood of such a possibility in Dallas.

As chairman of the Mayor's Youth Opportunity Committee, Morris mobilized the Dallas Chamber of Commerce and Dallas Junior Chamber of Commerce, which together lined up commitments for summer employment from more than 550 Dallas businesses. The first Job Fair, held in May 1968 at the Women's Building at Fair Park, attracted more than 4,000 Dallas area teens and young adults. More than 3,500 people lined up summer jobs that same day, a stunning result hailed by the Texas Employment Commission and the Urban League.

Another of Morris' major undertakings as Chamber of Commerce president came in the area of education. Dallas led all other U.S. metropolitan areas in job formation in the 1960s, and Hite and other city leaders wanted to ensure its future growth.

By 1968, Hite had taken to calling Dallas/Fort Worth the "brainpower center" of the Southwest. "There are more Ph.D's employed by industry in Dallas than in any other Southwestern or Southern city. There are more master's degrees in Dallas industry than in any other Southwestern or Southern city. In today's technological society, business growth depends upon brainpower. That's why, between 1960 and 1967, Dallas enjoyed the greatest growth of any of the nation's 20 largest metropolitan areas. That is why Dallas has only 1.5 percent unemployment compared to a national average of 3.7 percent."

Morris Hite's efforts in higher education focused on having a branch of the University of Texas system established in Dallas. Hite served on the advisory council of the Southwest Center for Advanced Studies (SCAS), a private research center founded and funded by several of the top executives at Texas Instruments, including Eugene McDermott, Cecil Green and Erik Jonsson. Hite helped them hatch a plan whereby SCAS would be converted from private to public status, through a metamorphosis into the University of Texas-Dallas (UTD).

The irony couldn't be overlooked: Morris Hite, high school dropout, at the forefront for higher education in North Texas. But Morris knew that by developing additional brainpower Dallas and the North Texas area would offer prospective employers a broader and deeper talent pool. The talent pool would appeal to both corporations looking to relocate headquarters or division operations and entrepreneurs planning new ventures. The vision Hite shared with Dallas leaders in the late 1960s could be seen two decades later, when the North Texas area was hailed in technology circles as "The Silicon Prairie," a reference to its prominence in the world of high-tech.

Getting the University of Texas-Dallas approved by the Texas Legislature proved to be easier articulated than accomplished. Morris Hite spent a good part of the spring of 1969 in Austin, working with legislators and legislative committees. The concept engendered controversy, filibusters and behind-the-scenes dealmaking, Texas-style.

In the end, the UTD camp had to compromise with the College Coordinating Board before Texas Gov. Preston Smith signed into law on June 13, 1969, House Bill 303, transforming SCAS into UTD. The compromise was that the University of Texas-Dallas would be primarily a graduate school, with only junior and senior level courses available to undergraduates. "I have the privilege of signing into law a bill that will substantially contribute to the cause and the system of higher education in Texas," Gov. Smith announced. "It is a measure that will soon make Dallas' educational dreams educational realities."

"This will give North Central Texas a balanced higher education system, complementing and supplementing our community college and private and public college for years to come," Hite told reporters. Privately, he told his associates at Tracy-Locke what an eye-opening experience the push for UTD had been. "I found out that education is much more political than politics," he said. "I have knots on my head and callouses on my knees to remind me that you have to work hard and bow low for anything you get in Austin."

Hite stepped down from his Chamber of Commerce position at the end of 1969, but his efforts to forge a new future for Dallas were neither overlooked nor soon forgotten. A committee of business leaders named Morris Hite the 1969 recipient of the Linz Award.

Dallas' oldest civic honor, the Linz Award is presented

annually to the Dallas County resident who provides the greatest benefit to the community without receiving any monetary compensation for the effort. The list of honorees reads like a who's who of people who built the city: Karl Hoblitzelle, Woodall Rogers, R.L. Thornton (both Sr. and Jr.), C.A. Tatum, Robert B. Cullum, Joe M. Dealey, John Stemmons.

The Linz Award selection committee cited Hite's leadership role both in the creation of the University of Texas at Dallas and the summer Job Fair. Hite accepted the award with typical humility. "I don't feel qualified to add my name to this august list," he said. "By giving me this award, you are giving this award to the business community of Dallas. I am convinced that the future depends on businessmen, not the government. Our problems will be solved by businessmen working together for the common good."

Hite had become accustomed to picking up awards. The North Texas chapter of the American Marketing Association named him "Marketing Man of the Year" in 1967, and the Dallas Advertising League presented him with the 1969 Silver Medal for distinguished service.

But those other awards had come from his business colleagues. The Linz Award validated Morris' contribution to his city and his fellow man. It removed any question that Morris Hite was more than an adman.

CHAPTER THIRTEEN

"IF PEOPLE WANT TO BUY THIS DAMN SERVICE, WHY DON'T WE SELL IT TO THEM?" —MORRIS HITE

Dallas faced a crossroads in the mid-1960s and so did Tracy-Locke. Morris Hite, freed from much of his hands-on duties with existing ad accounts, had time to ponder the big picture for the ad agency. Time to consider the future. Time to plan.

As he pondered and mulled, Hite began to see the possibility for building Tracy-Locke into a total communications company with operations in advertising and allied fields like marketing research, public relations, broadcasting and commercial production. The ad agency would remain as the linchpin, of course, but Tracy-Locke would expand and grow by diversifying its operations.

Hite put his plan in motion in April 1965, setting up the first Tracy-Locke subsidiary company, Marketing and Research Counselors, Inc., or M/A/R/C. Client Roland Baird of Mrs Baird's Bakeries, who more than a decade earlier had scoffed when Hite showed him an unsolicited market analysis, had since become the agency's best user of research. Baird's ringing endorsement of Tracy-Locke's research capability ultimately led to the formation of M/A/R/C, Hite explained.

"I'd go to cocktail parties and business luncheons and some guy would come up to me and say, "Morris, Roland Baird was telling me about a market research study you did for him and how it's been really helpful. We need someone to do a research study like that for us. Could you do it?'

"And I'd say 'No, this is a service we maintain just for advertising clients. Sorry.' But after this happened to me two or three times—if I had been real smart it would have occurred to me after the first time—I said to myself, 'Gee, Hite, if people want to buy this damn service, why don't we sell it to them?'"

Morris spent one weekend at home drawing up plans for the new company. He realized that M/A/R/C—he thought of the name himself—would have to operate separate and apart from Tracy-Locke. Confidentiality is paramount in marketing research, where a CIA-type mentality seems to be part of the package. Potential customers, ad agencies as well as national marketers, would balk if they thought Tracy-Locke personnel had access to the M/A/R/C files.

Hite wanted his longtime research ace, Jack Taylor, to head up M/A/R/C, but Taylor chose to stay on as the agency's director of research and media. So Morris hired an executive recruiter to conduct a search for M/A/R/C's first president; and the search led to Jan E. Muller. Morris liked the fact that Muller had worked both on the agency side of the ad business (BBDO in Chicago) and the client side (Toni hair care products). It gave an individual broader perspective on the potential uses for research.

Morris also hired Mildred Steindorf to head up field operations at M/A/R/C. Steindorf, who had coordinated the Dallas census in 1950 and 1960, was a popular and well-known figure in marketing research circles. She'd handled Texas and Southwest projects for many national companies based in New York and Chicago. They knew from experience they could count on "Millie" to deliver. Steindorf personally had trained a small legion of telephone interviewers, called the "kitchen corps," which M/A/R/C planned to employ for its data collection.

Muller, a Swedish native with thick accent and a Ph.D, had plenty of marketing research know-how, but little salesmanship. It quickly became clear to Hite and everyone else that Muller wasn't the right person for the job. Ninety days into Tracy-Locke's diversification program, Muller was out of a job and M/A/R/C's chances for survival seemed in jeopardy. Then Hite turned to an old associate, Bud Phillips, to bail him out.

Phillips had joined Clay Stephenson in Tracy-Locke's Houston office in late 1958. He left Clay Stephenson & Associates in the early 1960s and moved to Jackson, Mississippi, as advertising and research director at Dumas-Miller, manufacturers of Pine-Sol household cleaner. After Dumas-Miller was acquired by American Cyanamid, Phillips relocated to Wayne, New Jersey.

When Morris tracked him down in the summer of '65, Bud expressed an eagerness in the job at M/A/R/C. Phillips, after all, had personally done most of the legwork and brainwork in Tracy-Locke's early research jobs. Phillips came back to Dallas and nursed M/A/R/C through its infancy. Most of the first research assignments came from Tracy-Locke clients, Frito-Lay in particular, but M/A/R/C began building accounts not affiliated with the ad agency. Texas banks and TV stations became two categories interested in research applications.

But Bud Phillips could see a need to expand M/A/R/C's scope of operations beyond Texas and the Southwest, where companies lagged behind their national counterparts in appreciating the applications and potential benefits of market research. M/A/R/C's future rested in the Northeast and Midwest with the megamarketers like General Foods, Procter & Gamble, General Mills.

To score with those accounts, M/A/R/C needed to develop an exclusive product, an attention-getting device. A real grabber, in other words. Phillips, working with Jack Taylor, who migrated over from the ad agency as executive vice president in '68, and Frank Smith, a former agency account man who became M/A/R/C's vice president of marketing in '69, devised what they called the "National Advertising Index."

The National Advertising Index drew on a random-digit national telephone sample (code name: TELNO) to measure the effectiveness of advertising campaigns and overall brand awareness. The methodology was a modification of the "How Much, How Good" surveys Tracy-Locke had been conducting since the mid-1950s.

M/A/R/C's new product represented a breakthrough in data collection. "Until then, nobody believed you could gather consumer research on the telephone," said Jack Taylor. "They thought all research had to be gathered door-to-door. But we conducted tests and determined our telephone data were just as valid."

M/A/R/C also capitalized on the advent of wide area telephone service, or WATS lines. The company paid a flat monthly fee for the phone service, and kept its interviewers busy six-and-a-half days a week. The operation proved cost-effective; what else was so nice for the price as being able to keep the phone lines going 13.5 hours a day? Americans suddenly began to pick up the telephone and hear the words: *"May I ask you a few questions about your shopping habits? Do you prefer brand X or brand Y. . . ."*

Frank Smith spent the better part of two years, 1969 and 1970, living out of a suitcase, lining up national business for M/A/R/C.

"The National Advertising Index got me in the door to a lot of companies, although we never actually sold that much of it. It generated other sales, though. I had a flip-chart presentation I used to make and a lot of times, the prospect would stop me half the way through and say 'That's interesting, but not really what I need. Can you do another kind of project for me, maybe a focus group or depth motivation study?' I'd say sure."

Some of the early subscribers to the National Advertising Index included Texaco, Anderson Clayton Foods, Gulf and Frito-Lay. To raise its visibility within the advertising world, M/A/R/C created a measurement of the "most popular TV campaigns." The publicity attracted interest, and assignments from many of the large New York agencies, including Dancer Fitzgerald Sample, SSC&B, Ogilvy & Mather, N.W. Ayer, Foote, Cone & Belding and BBDO.

M/A/R/C also built a client base for depth motivation research, open-ended, unstructured interviews that probe a consumers' conscious (sometimes sub-conscious) motives for purchasing decisions. Bud Phillips did much of the data interpretation and wrote the specific marketing strategies the research suggested.

With Smith hustling business, Steindorf directing the WATS operation, and Phillips and Taylor refining the research tools, M/A/R/C's customer base in the 1970s began to read like a who's who of American marketing. General Foods. R.J. Reynolds. Coca-Cola. H.J. Heinz & Co. A.T.& T.

M/A/R/C proved to be both the first, and most successful, Tracy-Locke spinoff. Two decades later, M/A/R/C ranked among the five largest market research companies in the United States. Its annual revenues had topped $50 million and its handsome headquarters building in Las Colinas, near Dallas-Fort Worth International Airport, bespoke the company's success.

M/A/R/C had come a long way, literally and figuratively, since Morris Hite sat down at the kitchen table at his house on Janmar Circle and drew up the plans for an independent research company on a winter day in 1965.

Diversification at Tracy-Locke continued in 1966 with the agency's purchase of KJIM-AM, an easy listening station in Fort Worth. Seemingly one station deserved another one, so Hite next bought KCNW-AM, a country and western station in Tulsa. The Tulsa acquisition included 31 acres of land near the prestigious Southern Hills Country Club. The land would make money for the company even after the station did not.

The agency's foray into radio put Morris at loggerheads with his national advertising colleagues. Hite didn't realize that the American Association of Advertising Agencies (4A's) expressly prohibited ad agencies from owning broadcast properties. The organization, of which Hite served as secretary-treasurer and a member of the board of directors, believed conflict of interest charges could easily be leveled against any agency that bought TV or radio stations. Concerned about the constant attacks on advertising's professionalism, the 4A's decided to nip one potential problem area in the bud.

"According to the by-laws of the 4A's, it is all right for me or any of our executives to own radio stations or other media," said a flabbergasted Morris Hite. " However, it is verboten for any company to own stations. The theory is that Tracy-Locke's ownership of media, even though it is through a subsidiary corporation, will cause us to lose objectivity in media selection."

Hite didn't agree with such thinking. "I wish John Crichton of the 4A's could have been present at the last meeting I had with George Faulder, who manages our two stations. George was quite incensed because he said he was getting very little business from our media department."

"George said he understood why I had cautioned all timebuyers to be very careful in buying time on our stations. In fact, I had told them never to buy unless they could support their buying decision in such a way that it could not be questioned by clients or competitive stations. George said he was aware of this. But he also said our timebuyers were being so extremely careful not to show favoritism that they had practically excluded him from their buying lists in both markets."

Hite noted the extreme discretion on the part of the agency's media department had given rival stations in Fort Worth and Tulsa an avenue to exploit. "George tells me that other stations tell advertisers, 'Look, those stations aren't any good. Tracy-Locke *owns* them and they won't even buy time on them for their own clients.'"

Push came to shove over the agency's radio ownership. The 4A's pushed Morris off the board and shoved Tracy-Locke out of the organization. But Hite remained undeterred with his plans to build a total communications company—4A's or no 4A's. By the early 1970s, Tracy-Locke Co. would add a design studio, film processing lab, public relations arm, personnel consulting company and an auto leasing operation. And when the 4A's relaxed its restriction on media ownership and invited Tracy-Locke to reaffiliate, Hite assured them he'd "give it serious thought."

Along with Tracy-Locke's diversification program in the 1960s came geographic expansion. The opening of a San Antonio office to service Pearl triggered a growth period that by the end of the decade saw Tracy-Locke operating in five cities.

But where Morris Hite embraced diversification, he harbored doubts and misgivings about geographic expansion. He believed branch offices diluted the head office's *control.* Hite knew how Joe Dawson and Shelley Tracy headed off to New York with the Conoco business and never came back. He'd seen Clay Stephenson head off to Houston with Duncan Coffee Co. and never come back. Those chapters in Tracy-Locke's history made Morris reluctant to embrace branch offices.

On the other hand, Hite liked new business. And if a branch office represented the difference in whether or not

Tracy-Locke landed a significant account, Morris had but one question: "Where can I lease some office space?"

In late 1967, Tracy-Locke landed the Frontier Airlines business in Denver after Frontier acquired another regional carrier, Central Airlines. Tracy-Locke had serviced Central Airlines, which operated out of Meacham Field in Fort Worth, for a couple of years. It competed for the combined ad account against Frontier's incumbent agency, Kenyon & Eckhardt.

A key element of Tracy-Locke's presentation, delivered by Morris Hite, Fred Rowe and Marshall Bateman, centered on the agency's pledge to open a branch office in Denver. The agency also promised not to solicit any other business for 12 months. The service commitment apparently swayed Frontier's agency review committee, though Bateman, who set up shop in Denver in December 1967, observed, "We used to joke that Frontier kept its law firm and C.P.A. and let Central keep its ad agency."

Earlier in 1967, Tracy-Locke had reopened a branch office in Houston. Richard Brown, a University of Houston grad, headed up the office, which handled three separate Pearl distributorships in the greater Houston area. The agency also handled Imperial Sugar, based in nearby Sugar Land. And, for the third separate time in the agency's history, it handled the Comet Rice account.

In late 1968, Tracy-Locke gained the national account of The Borden Co. previously handled by Young & Rubicam. Hite asked Bill James, the head of the San Antonio office, to be the management representative in New York and dispatched Don Schultz as account supervisor. Failing health prevented account man Herb Lehmann, who had serviced Borden for well over a decade, from making the move.

By the end of the 1960s, Tracy-Locke operated branch offices in San Antonio, Houston, Denver and New York, in addition to headquarters in Dallas. Immediately ahead in its future were openings of branch offices in San Francisco and Columbus, Ohio. From roughly 40 employees and $10 million in billings in 1960, the ad agency had grown to nearly 200 employees and $27 million in billings in 1969.

For the second time in the agency's history, Tracy-Locke had a presence in New York. Schultz and the others on the Borden account hung their hats at an office on Park Avenue between 48th and 49th street. But for Morris Hite, Manhattan remained uncharted territory. At times he expressed regrets over never having worked in New York, never having measured himself against the Bill Bernbachs and David Ogilvys and Raymond Rubicams and Rosser Reeveses—enduring names of American advertising. At other times, Hite expressed the view that nobody on Madison Avenue knew any more about the business than he did. No brag, just fact.

Experience with accounts like Frito-Lay and Borden gave Morris first-hand dealings with New York agencies and, if anything, he felt the Madison Avenue boys took a superficial approach to understanding their clients' sales problems. They didn't *dig*. "Hell, I've been in meetings with the Young & Rubicam people and I guarantee they don't know how the milk business operates," he'd say. (On the other hand, Young & Rubicam did create the company's enduring spokesbovine, Elsie The Cow.)

Hite, like most ad executives who lived and worked outside New York, took pot-shots at the Manhattan mystique. As he said in a radio interview with KRLD-AM in Dallas in 1966:

"There's no Madison Avenue atmosphere in Dallas. We import some Madison Avenue folks, but try to make them into Texans." Asked how to spot a Madison Avenue type, Hite replied, "By the Brooks Brothers suit—tight-fitting, natural shoulders—and by a manner of talking that never does get down to reality."

In the same interview, Hite stamped himself as somewhat other than on the cutting edge of women's role in advertising. "Some of the nation's biggest advertisers sell their products to women, and we find women copywriters very effective. Women are best in the creative areas of advertising. We don't have much luck with them as account executives."

The status of women at Tracy-Locke would begin to change in the 1970s. Along with everything else.

CHAPTER FOURTEEN

"THE INSIDE JOKE WAS THAT IF YOU WANTED TO GET PROMOTED AT TRACY-LOCKE YOU HAD TO LOSE SOME IMPORTANT BUSINESS." —MORRIS HITE

In the early 1970s, Morris Hite entered the transitional phase of his advertising career. Having reached his 60s, Hite realized he needed to allow for the line of succession at the agency.

Neither of Hite's sons, having just entered their 20s, showed any interest in following their dad. Lee, a graduate of the University of Texas, went to work at the agency's sister company, M/A/R/C, but his interests and aptitudes were in computer systems and computer programming, not advertising. Jerry, a cum laude graduate of Stanford University, chose to become a writer of prose, not ad copy. Neither shared his father's zeal for the business. Nor did any of Morris' three daughters, Sissy, Florence or Aimee, figure to blaze trails in advertising.

Morris would have to look beyond his immediate family to find an heir apparent for Tracy-Locke, but he wouldn't have to look too far. The obvious choices to succeed him were three of the agency's most accomplished account people: Bob Brown, Norm Campbell and Stewart Mitchell. Experienced, aggressive, in their late 30s (Campbell and Brown) or early 40s (Mitchell), each possessed qualities that made him a contender for the job.

Brown had spent most of the 1960s in San Antonio. He worked as the supervisor on the Pearl account and succeeded Bill James as the head of the San Antonio office when Hite tapped James for Borden duty in New York. Brown had brought in new business like Friedrich heating and air conditioning and Volkswagen Southwest division, some 120 dealerships in a nine-state area. The San Antonio office made major contributions to Tracy-Locke's profit picture.

Campbell had joined Tracy-Locke in 1965, after several years in New York with BBDO. A native Texan, he had returned to Dallas only to leave again in 1968 when he replaced Marshall Bateman in Denver. Campbell had built up the office, servicing the anchor client, Frontier Airlines, and adding new business.

Mitchell, meanwhile, had been at Tracy-Locke headquarters in Dallas since 1959. Mitchell supervised two of the agency's mainstay accounts, Interfirst and Frito-Lay. When Hite went on sabbatical at the Dallas Chamber of Commerce in 1968 and 1969, Stewart stepped forward as the number two in command. Many observers both inside and outside the agency thought Stewart eventually would be Morris' successor.

In Hite's absence for civic duties, relations between Brown, Campbell and Mitchell not unexpectedly became cool. Brown and Campbell were accustomed to running their own shows and didn't cotton to the idea of reporting to anyone other than Hite. Having to relay messages to Hite through Mitchell made them feel lower on the corporate rung.

To smooth things out, Brown and Campbell began commuting from their respective branch cities to Dallas, where the agency occupied new offices on Main Street. Tracy-Locke had moved into the Metropolitan Savings building in downtown Dallas in 1969, having outgrown its building on Central Expressway and deciding to sell the property rather than renovate.

Morris deliberately took a passive role in the management transition. He knew the trio would have to work things out themselves. An autocratic decision on his part would have been detrimental to the cause.

In the spring of '71, the question of agency succession came to a head. Brown, Campbell and Mitchell retreated for what came to be known at the agency as the "Summit in Santa Fe." Over the course of a working weekend, they mapped out a strategy for the agency's future and a delineation of responsibilities for themselves. They returned to Dallas and made these recommendations to Morris:

That each would be named executive vice president. That Campbell would oversee corporate development; that Mitchell would oversee account services; that Brown would oversee creative and administrative services.

"I'll buy all that," said Hite.

They also told Morris that Campbell seemed the natural choice to succeed him as president and should be groomed as such.

"Let me sleep on that," said Hite.

While the agency prepared for a changing of the guard, Morris Hite concerned himself with corporate responsibilities. He began preparations for taking Tracy-Locke Co. public. To assist with the financial arrangements, Hite hired O.T. "Tom" Forman, Jr. as chief financial officer.

Forman, who came from Recognition Equipment, not only brought new financial discipline to Tracy-Locke, he added experience with computers that the rapidly growing company needed. When he wasn't working on the prospectus and other matters associated with going public, Forman set up systems on the computer to enhance accounting and financial control. He'd uncovered some problems with accounts receivable that required immediate attention. The company's growth required more financial sophistication than Morris' roughing out figures on a cocktail napkin, something he'd done for years.

Tracy-Locke Co. took its stock public on December 17,

1971. Schneider, Bernet & Hickman, a Dallas-based brokerage house, handled the public offering of 150,000 shares at $12 a share asked, $11.50 bid. Tracy-Locke Co. put up 62,500 shares, while Morris sold 87,500 shares from his personal holdings. After brokerage fees and commissions, the proceeds from the sale read Tracy-Locke Co.—$694,000; Morris Hite—$971,000.

It made for a very Merry Christmas around the Hite household. After the sale, Morris still held 25.7 percent of the agency common stock outstanding, or roughly 100,000 of 400,000 shares.

The public offering served several purposes. One, it allowed Hite to get a large chunk of money out of the agency and begin some estate planning. Two, it reduced Hite's concentration so that in the case of unforeseen circumstances other members of the company could buy out his shares. Three, it created a market value for the Tracy-Locke shares, all of which were employee-owned.

By 1972, the agency's diversification program had extended to include Point Inc., a graphics design company, and World Broadcasting System, a radio and television syndications and service business. The company looked at several more radio properties for future acquisitions and expansion into film processing.

Tracy-Locke's revenues reached $6.4 million in 1971, and nearly 40 percent came from the subsidiary companies. Hite told the Dallas press that though TLC had plans to be a "broad-based company" it had no plans to make acquisitions outside the communications field. He didn't have the inclination to try to be another Jim Ling, the Dallas entrepreneur whose far-flung acquisitions added the word "conglomerate" to the vocabulary of American business. (Ling's base company, LTV Corp., had been a Tracy-Locke client.)

In February 1972, with the agency basking in the afterglow of record earnings and its recent public offering, and with agency employees scanning the financial news page for the over-the-counter (symbol: TLC), Tracy-Locke suffered its first case of the most feared affliction in the ad agency world: the 'Adios' syndrome.

On Feb. 1, Pearl Beer announced it was taking its ad account, which included the budget for Country Club Malt Liquor, in house. On the heels of that announcement came word that the Southwest Volkswagen distributors planned to head back to Doyle Dane Bernbach, which handled the national VW business. Next came word from Denver that relations with Frontier Airlines were on the wane and that the carrier planned to replace Tracy-Locke with a local agency, Frye-Sills.

The three account losses had not been totally unexpected. Agencies and clients alike know when a relationship reaches the end. Hite assured his stockholders that the company had taken appropriate measures to contain costs. "We've already cut back personnel and we're aggressively soliciting new business," he said. "Losing those two may keep us from having an excellent growth year, but it shouldn't cause us to make less money than we did last year." Brave words, indeed.

Hite's statement about cutting back on personnel reflects a reality of the adworld: *When major accounts desert an agency, staff reductions aren't far behind.*

That's one reason why security-conscious young people need to steer clear of the advertising business, especially if their career aspirations include a 25-year service pin or a 30-year gold watch. A career in advertising, especially on the agency side, often means three or four moves before settling in at one shop. To move up, you usually have to move out.

Many ad agencies adhere to a 50-30-20 ratio for revenues. They allocate 50 percent of revenues to salary, 30 percent to overhead (rent, equipment leasing, and other costs), and earmark 20 percent for profit. When revenues decline abruptly and precipitously—when a big client fires your agency—it's much easier to slash your payroll than renegotiate the lease on your plush executive offices.

A few altruistic agencies will carry employees on the payroll after a significant account loss, but it's a luxury few can afford. And fewer still elect to do. The economic reality of advertising is that keeping your job often means keeping your accounts. It adds to the neurosis and paranoia permeating ad agency life. So it goes.

The Pearl account, once the best piece of business in the house, had begun losing steam by the early 1970s. Rocketed by the success of Tracy-Locke's "water story" campaign and the agency's sales promotion skills, Pearl maintained its position as Texas' best-selling brand in the early to mid-1960s.

Symbolic of the account's success story was a three-dimensional billboard Tracy-Locke created for Pearl and leased on a high-visibility location on Stemmons Freeway near downtown Dallas. The billboard carried the "Country of 1,100 Springs" line and showed a waterfall scene next to a can of the product. Agency artist Ben Mead created the award-winning billboard that became a favorite for pranksters who'd fill the water with soap or dyes.

In the 1950s and 1960s, regional brands began falling prey as national breweries began decentralizing operations. A growth market like Texas, with its expanding population and relatively high per capita consumption, offered a prime target for expansion. Before you could say Andrew Fabacher, Anheuser-Busch had built a brewery in Houston, Schlitz in Longview and Miller in Fort Worth.

Just as McDonald's Corp. took its 19-cent hamburgers and golden arches nationwide in the early 1960s, rendering the Mom-and-Pop malt shop obsolete, the national breweries launched the beer wars of the '60s. In the life-and-death struggle for the baby boomer market, or Foam

Over America, regional breweries suddenly started appearing on the list of endangered species. Especially as the price differential on the product narrowed. The five-cent spread on premium brands became a smaller consideration as retail prices increased.

Morris Hite probably had seen the future back in 1954, when he helped introduce Budweiser to Texas. Given the green light from August Busch, Hite returned to Dallas and produced an 8-second ID spot for Budweiser. It featured a six-pack of Bud held by a buxom blonde in western wear who said: "Best Tastin' Beer in Texas, I Said Best Tastin'." What it lacked in originality it made up for in hard-sell.

If the external strategies from the national companies didn't exert enough pressure on Pearl, the internal strategies of the Pearl management did. Over the protests of Tracy-Locke, Pearl decided to shelve its "water story" campaign and go with an up-tempo, lifestyle advertising geared to the youth market.

It amounted to spitting into the wind. Tracy-Locke's research identified the culprit: teen rebellion. Pearl's management failed to appreciate that the '60s youth didn't want to emulate his parents. If the old man drank a regional brand like Pearl, then Junior sure as hell wanted to drink a Bud or a Schlitz. (Only Coors managed to escape the stigma of a regional, gaining '60s cult status as a Rocky Mountain high.) Pearl's new strategy captured no new youthful drinkers and drove away some loyal Pearl drinkers.

Tracy-Locke tried to blunt the success of the national labels by positioning Pearl as a premium beer. In a campaign called "Straight Talk," the agency wrote ads claiming Pearl put more man-hours in its brewing process than Bud or Schlitz. "Which is the premium beer?" asked the ads. But comparative advertising, which came to the fore in the early 1980s, was verboten in the 1960s. Schlitz complained to the Federal Communications Commission and Tracy-Locke had to revise its campaign.

The agency was also ahead of its time with light beer. Hoping to boost the sagging fortunes at Pearl, Tracy-Locke showed its innovation by working with the Pearl chemists to develop a product called Pearl Premium Light. It had fewer calories, less alcohol and an altogether lighter taste than Pearl's flagship brand. Tracy-Locke designed the label, produced point-of-sale pieces and did test marketing for Pearl Premium Light. The agency believed the category showed immense potential.

Pearl management turned a cold shoulder to the idea. "Why the hell would we want to support another brand, when we can't sell the one we've got?" came their reply. Famous last words, especially since by the late 1970s the hottest word in beer consumption was light. Or lite.

By the early 1970s, relationship between Pearl and Tracy-Locke had grown threadbare. It's a common occurrence in advertising, although it seldom happened during Morris Hite's tenure. After yet another managment change at Pearl, the new bosses wanted to reposition the brand as an upscale. "Hell," spat Hite, "Pearl's a redneck beer. Everybody knows that much. Or ought to." The agency produced new TV spots aimed at redneck, blue collar drinkers and the Pearl brass blanched when they saw the work.

The friction over such a fundamental question as the target market grew worse when Pearl decided to become a major sponsor of "Opera Under the Stars" in Houston. Hell's bells, argued Hite, the opera crowd drinks champagne or wine. If they go slumming and have a beer, it's generally an imported beer. They sure don't give a damn about Pearl beer.

Morris knew Pearl would be better off sponsoring the dances at Gilley's, the country-and-western club in the Houston suburb of Pasadena than the opera. Pearl had, in fact, staked out the redneck market early in the 1960s. Bob Brown produced a series of Pearl radio commercials with country music artists like Willie Nelson, Webb Pierce, and Faron Young.

But Pearl had long since surrendered that particular niche to its crosstown rival, Lone Star. During the mid-to-late 1970s, during the rise of Texas chic and "redneck rock," Lone Star beer sold a lot of barrels through its strong positioning with rednecks. Did the opera buffs come forward to bolster Pearl's sales? Take a guess.

The loss of Pearl and the other accounts shook Tracy-Locke to its foundation, triggering the long-awaited, much-anticipated managment change. Norm Campbell took over as agency president in June 1972. Even though Morris raised the issue of whether he should surrender the reins with the agency in such bad shape, the Tracy-Locke board felt the onus to rebuild the agency should be shared by Campbell, Mitchell and Brown.

Noting the rise of Campbell and Brown on the heels of the departure of Frontier Airlines and Pearl, Hite observed, "For a time, the inside joke was if you wanted to get promoted at Tracy-Locke you had to lose an important account."

But agency hands had little to laugh about in the fall of 1972. The best word to describe new business development was moribund. Campbell chased one $20,000 account just so he could feel he was doing something to give the agency some momentum.

At Christmas, Campbell had to play the role of Ebenezer Scrooge. He announced to the staff there'd be no Christmas bonuses and no across-the-board pay increases. Tracy-Locke's billings for 1972 had totaled $29.7 million, down from $32.7 million in 1971. Not the trend a new agency president likes to see.

But in February 1973, one year after the Pearl defection, Tracy-Locke got hot. Johns Manville tapped the Denver office for corporate advertising, a quick $2 million budge. LTV Corp. subsidiary Wilson Foods, a meat packing company in Oklahoma City, climbed aboard. Another $1 million-plus. Texas International Airlines flew in. Another seven-figure account.

And so it went. In one incredible stretch of new business prowess, Norm Campbell and Bob Brown pitched nine accounts and won nine consecutive times. When one agency staffer wondered aloud how the agency could digest all the new business, Brown replied: "We'll string 'em up. You clean them."

Then in May 1973, Tracy-Locke landed the $6 million account of Phillips Petroleum, previously housed with J. Walter Thompson in New York. According to the advertising trade press, it represented the largest single account acquisition by an agency in the South or Southwest.

Tracy-Locke went head-to-head in a final showdown with Tatham, Laird & Kudner of Chicago. The Bartlesville, Okla.-based oil company had earlier sized up various national agencies. Morris Hite later told friends that winning the Phillips account signified that Tracy-Locke could compete with the big national agencies for major accounts. It represented another benchmark in the agency's history.

Significantly, the Phillips Petroleum pitch had been Norm Campbell's show all the way. Norm's schedule called for him to join Hite in mid-March at a Borden Co. managers' meeting in Florida, until he received a call from Joe Downing, the Phillips ad manager. Downing was coming to Dallas and would like to meet with Campbell. Could that be arranged?

You bet. Norm canceled his Florida plans and briefed Morris on the opportunity with Phillips. "The hardest thing I ever had to do in advertising was to stay out of the pitch," said Hite, but he knew the business belonged in Campbell's bailiwick.

When Norm met with Phillips ad and marketing officials for a briefing on how the final competition with Tathum-Laird would be set up, he told Downing and the others, "Okay, from today on, we're going to act like we already have your account." In the ensuing weeks, he dispatched a steady stream of staffers to Bartlesville. The group consisted of one or more of the following: Jim Brady and Dick Craiglow from account service; Howard Englander from creative; Don Mitchum from research; Jerry Still from media. Campbell went whenever he could.

The strategy paid dividends. "We established a chemistry with the people at Phillips that was instrumental to our ultimate selection," said Campbell. By contrast, the Tatham-Laird executives did not reappear in Bartlesville until the final pitch.

Norm invited Morris to witness the final presentation to Phillips and Hite couldn't say no. He went along and watched Campbell serve as ringmaster during a show with several acts. Afterward Hite told his protege, "Norm, I wouldn't have done one goddamn thing the way you did it. But I'll tell you something else, I wouldn't have made as good a presentation as you did, either."

For all of Hite's gifts as a salesman, marketer and Big Idea Hunter, some associates insisted his greatest talent was bringing out the best in others.

"Having delegated the responsibility and authority of president to me he never second-guessed the agency's operations," said Campbell. "He didn't try to usurp my position. But he was always available to me to any degree I wanted. He played an especially important role with the long-time accounts like Borden, Haggar and Imperial. You bet I wanted him involved. But otherwise it was a clean cut."

When Tracy-Locke celebrated its 60th anniversary in September 1973, the agency bubbled with enthusiasm. So did the parent holding company.

M/A/R/C/ had capitalized on the trend to focus group studies and had introduced a technique for identifying cluster groups based on shoppers' prospensity-to-buy. More than 90 percent of M/A/R/C's business came from outside Tracy-Locke. The research company kept 48 WATS lines humming while conducting 3,000 interviews in an average week.

The company had cut a deal with Tecor, Inc. to acquire a film processing company called PSI. Managed by previous owner Robert Redd, PSI contributed to the overall profit picture. The only operating unit that didn't make much money for Tracy-Locke was broadcast. The company started to purchase another radio station, but changed its mind in mid-1973 and subsequently decided to get out of the business. "We knew how to buy radio time," Hite observed wistfully. "We just never did a very good job of selling it."

Hite had never been too personally involved in the radio operations, other than to write editorials for KJIM-AM in Fort Worth. He hoped to use that forum to spark civic pride. He felt Cowtown lacked Dallas' "can-do" spirit.

With the Norm Campbell era underway at the ad agency and the subsidiary operations contributing to the bottom line, Hite could pick and choose his activities. One of his pet projects involved KERA-TV, the public broadcasting outlet in North Texas.

During his Chamber of Commerce days in the late 1960s, Morris had helped raise corporate funds to support the fledgling operation. He hosted a series of luncheons at his own expense at which the station's executives could interact with Dallas business leaders.

Some of the luncheons resembled close encounters of the worst kind. Many members of the conservative Dallas business community fumed over the PBS programming, be it the local newscast, called "Newsroom" (featuring Jim Lehrer) or syndicated shows like "Black Journal." The Dallas establishment branded PBS variously as maverick journalism, a mouthpiece for liberalism or something more contemptuous.

Hite didn't share their view, however. "Morris had an independent turn of mind," recalled Robert Wilson, KERA's general manager. "He never waivered in his support of our programming initiatives. He'd stand up and take the heat and pressure. Morris had a basic understanding of what broadcasting should be . . . that the freedom of choice should ultimately rest with the viewer."

Wilson recalled how Hite backed his decision to air a documentary called "Banks and The Poor," which attacked the banking industry for its lending policies to so-called "redlined" neighborhoods and communities.

"I've never seen such a well-orchestrated pressure campaign," said Wilson. "We heard from the American Bankers Association, the Texas Bankers Association, every lobbyist in America who represents banking interests. But Morris agreed we should go ahead with plans to air the show.

"Morris wasn't exactly crazy about the program content himself, but he knew a larger issue was involved. It was a gutsy call on his part, especially when you remember that First National Bank was one of his agency's accounts. But Morris always figured that somehow things would even out. That if one show didn't have the slant for a particular mindset, the next one would."

Another piece of unfinished business left over from Morris' Chamber days involved having Dallas-Fort Worth classified as a single Standard Metropolitan Statistical Area (SMSA). After some healing of old wounds, leaders in the two cities presented a united front to government officials. Separately, Dallas ranked 16th and Fort Worth 42nd but together they were 10th. "Those [SMSA] figures are the first thing business executives look at when they start considering a relocation or building a new plant. And this area has an exciting story to tell. It's growing faster than the nation or the rest of the state," said Hite.

To call attention to the Dallas-Fort Worth area, businessmen formed the North Texas Commission. Tracy-Locke landed the group's ad account and Harvie Chapman of the agency's public relations unit coined the term "Southwest Metroplex" (Metropolitan Complex) to describe it. Tracy-Locke built its first campaign around the advantages of locating next to Dallas-Fort Worth airport.

Hite also remained closely involved with the progress of the University of Texas at Dallas, which he helped shepherd through the Texas Legislature. Morris served on the university board and took an active part in development work. In 1985, UTD established the Morris Hite Center for Product Development and Marketing Science.

By the mid-1970s, Morris eased back on his business agenda. He and Caroline began scheduling more frequent trips abroad. He particularly enjoyed browsing in European castles while Caroline went shopping.

In a letter to his son, Jerry, detailing a trip in 1977 to Scandinavia and the Soviet Union, Morris told a story about the lack of enterprise he encountered in Russia. Parts of the countryside near Leningrad had reminded him of the stark illustrations in Grimm's Fairy Tales.

". . . [in Moscow], they have what they call Dollar stores. These stores are operated for tourists and accept hard currencies such as the U.S. dollar, German mark, English pound, etc. I spent some time in the book section of one of these stores looking for a book on Byzantine art. I finally found something that was reasonably close to what I wanted.

"Just as I had made up my mind, a young lady clerk tapped me on the shoulder and explained that it was 4 o'clock and the store was closing. I said, 'That's all right, I have made my selection. I would like to buy this book.' Her reply was, 'I'm sorry, we are closing. You will have to come back tomorrow.'"

Morris explained that he was part of a travel group scheduled to leave Moscow that evening. He would not be able to return the next day. He must make the purchase that very minute. Sorry, she said. Business hours were over. Those were the rules.

"The book cost about $20, so it was something more than a nuisance sale," wrote Hite. "I think this is a good example of what happens when people have no incentive. In an American bookstore, the clerk probably would have been on a commission and interested in making the sale. Even if she wasn't on commission, her supervisor would have made certain the customer was accommodated."

Hite knew all about keeping customers accommodated. "Advertising always gets back to being innovative and creative," he said. "My definition of creativity is a little broader than the guys in the creative department define it. Being creative is not just writing a good ad or a good commercial, but thinking of all the things necessary to sell an account. And even beyond that, the things necessary to help make their business grow."

Add all those things together and they spell account service.

CHAPTER FIFTEEN

"TO MRS. MUFOOSKY, THE COMMERCIALS MAY SEEM AS LONG AS A WHORE'S DREAM. BUT TO THE NEW ADVERTISER WHO HAS SPENT 100 Gs FOR HIS FIRST NETWORK COMMERCIAL—HE GETS A NEW UNDERSTANDING OF A SPLIT SECOND. IT'S THE FASTEST HALF MINUTE IN HIS LIFETIME."—MORRIS HITE

Account service, the relationship between an ad agency and its individual clients, can be considered advertising's alpha and omega, its beginning and end. Indeed, account service has provided the basis on which many relationships have begun. And fivefold more have ended because of it.

Disagreements over marketing strategy and tactics, advertising goals and objectives, creative approaches, compensation—compensation especially—have been known to undermine account service and, ultimately, the agency/client relationship. All too often the cause can be traced to unrealistic expectations.

Either the client believes advertising can accomplish more than it is capable of, or agency executives make assurances that advertising can deliver more than it can. Whichever, the clients become disillusioned and frustrated by the lack of results. Once that happens, all the conference reports or memos in the world can't cover your ass. Or save it.

In the advertising world, small bruises and nicks

sustained in the normal course of doing business can become festering sores. An oversight here, a slip up there often leads to discontent. Suddenly an agency/client relationship built on *we* turns into *us* against *them*. Though agencies and clients toss around such words as "teammates" and "partners" like advertising is an athletic competition, the simple truth is that few agencies and clients practice what they preach.

The ad press, not surprisingly, tends to place a premium on size. *ADWEEK, Ad Age* and other trade magazines compile and publish statistics on the billings of U.S. ad agencies as though size is the best barometer of agency performance. Many companies searching for an agency to handle their account tend to equate quantity (size) with quality (ability). That pernicious fact of ad life discriminates against smaller shops.

The "Bigger Is Better" mentality in advertising got pushed aside briefly during the Creative Revolution of the 1960s when the "creative boutiques" had their heyday. Size meant less than the strength of the creative reel. The mid-1980s also represented an up period for creative hot shops and hotshots, as industry attention focused on agencies like Chiat/Day in Los Angeles, Fallon-McElligott in Minneapolis, The Martin Agency in Richmond, The Richards Group in Dallas. But by the late 1980s, the pendulum swung back to size. The biggest news in U.S. advertising concerned mergers and consolidations, and the creation of mega-agencies.

The biggest agencies, not necessarily the best, are clustered in New York and Chicago. But who's to say the best creative work in American advertising can't come from Minneapolis or Seattle or Raleigh? And who's to say the best account service can't be done in Boston, St. Louis or Dallas? As Morris Hite liked to point out, good ideas and good thinking have no geographical constraints.

Maybe a better gauge of agency effectiveness than

sheer size of billings or a creative reputation would be: *How long does an agency keep its clients?* The history of American advertising tells us it's that clients won't keep their ad agencies around if:

A) They don't like the people working on their account;

B) They don't think their advertising sells products and makes them money.

Consider, then, that Morris Hite kept some of his clients in the shop for *more than four decades*. And that clients like Mrs Baird's, Imperial Sugar and Haggar stayed with Tracy-Locke even as generations of Bairds, Kempners and Haggars passed through the executive suite.

Why? Hite's clients liked him, respected him, trusted him. They liked the way he shot straight with them. They liked the fact his brand of account service never became obsequious; they also liked the fact Morris never used a words like 'obsequious' when 'ass-kisser' would do.

"Morris had a disarming honesty," observed Bob Brown. "When a new client first got to know him they'd wonder: *Is this guy for real?* They were used to having bad experiences with the b.s. types in the ad business and they weren't prepared for someone who gave it to them straight.

"Morris frequently wouldn't tell the client what the client wanted to hear. But he never, never lied to them."

Clients also liked Hite for his smarts. He knew a lot about their business and sales problems, but he didn't act like a know-it-all. Said Raymond Duvall, sales manager of Borden's dairy division: "Morris was a good listener. Unlike a lot of admen, he didn't do all the talking all the time. He listened carefully to get your side of the story. He wanted to know what *you* had to say."

Hite inspired confidence in clients because he approached their business with confidence. No matter the problem, Morris found a way cut to the core. "He had an ability to break off the periphery issues and cut straight to the heart. He didn't go off on tangents," said Dan Pollick, an agency account man.

Or as Bob Brown said, "Morris believed that this is a pretty simple business. You identify the problems advertising can help solve, you create ads designed to correct the problems, you expose the ads as effectively as possible and you evaluate the effectiveness of the ads against some predetermined standard of measurement."

Such a sharp focus helps a person keep perspective in a business where no "right" or "wrong" way of doing business exists. Ad strategies and their supporting campaigns are either good, real good or not-so-good.

Hite also had a knack for saying the right thing. Take the time Morris sold the Haggar family on buying network TV for the first time. He scheduled a $30,000 participation for Haggar on the ABC network for two western programs, "Sugarfoot" and "Bronco." TV westerns were then coming to the fore—"Bonanza," "Gunsmoke" and "Have Gun Will Travel" ranked among the top-rated shows—and did a good job of delivering the male audience Haggar sought as its prime target.

"First I had to beat on the network some," Hite recalled. "The old man [J.M. Haggar Sr.] thought it was like buying piece goods, so I had to squeeze the last nickel out of the deal. I had to get the network to give us sponsor bulletin at the beginning of the show and to promise to run the spot in the first five minutes of the program. That was in case the show turned out to be a turkey and viewers changed channels to another program.

"Finally came the night of the show. I'm at home in front of my TV. Larry DuPont, who wrote and produced the spot, is in front of his TV. Paul Rafferty, the account man on Haggar, is home in front of his TV. And the whole Haggar family has gathered together at the old man's house to watch the show.

"And I'm thinking to myself 'Godalmighty, all this

work and they'll screw it up somehow.' Either they'll forget the goddamn dealer tag, or the commercial will come on upside down or some damn thing will go wrong."

The "Bronco" program came on. The Haggar name appeared at the beginning as a sponsor's bulletin. At the first commercial break, the Haggar commercial appeared on the screen, the video rightside up, no glitches in the audio. At the end of the spot the dealer tag, which gives viewers information on where they can purchase Haggar slacks, came on the screen as planned.

"Everything went perfectly," said Hite. "I leaned back in my chair and said 'Thank God that's over with.'"

Just then the phone rang at the Hite residence.

"Morris?" a voice boomed, "Ed Haggar." Ed was the older of the two Haggar boys working at the company. He was the one in charge of the advertising and marketing.

"How're you doing, Ed?"

"Morris, did you see our TV commercial?"

"Yes, Ed, I saw it."

"Well . . . have you had any reaction to it yet?"

"As a matter of fact, I have," said Morris. "Caroline saw it. And she thinks it's great."

"Well, I've had some reaction, too," said Ed Haggar.

"Oh really? From who?"

"My dad."

"Well, what did he say?" asked Hite.

"He said, 'My God... thirty thousand dollars for *that*.'"

Hite knew a way to stop J.M. Haggar Sr.'s heart from palpitating. He took the client an A.C. Neilsen rating that showed the spot on "Bronco" had been seen by 17 million viewers. At a cost of $30,000 for the spot, it meant they'd reached their target market for an approximate cost of *two-tenths of a cent* per person. "That's a pretty cheap way to get your sales story out there," Morris told J.M. Haggar Sr.

Suddenly seeing the world through the eyes of his

adman, Haggar became a big supporter of television advertising. He especially enjoyed a Tracy-Locke TV ad for Haggar's line of wash-and-wear slacks. In the spot, called "Forever-Prest," a pair of Haggar slacks gets crumpled and wadded up and then flattened by a steamroller. But when held up to the camera, the slacks fall out wrinkle-free.

When that TV spot aired in the New York market, Gimbels sold out of Haggar slacks within 24 hours. The store frantically phoned Haggar with instructions to air freight thousands more pairs. The advertising gave Haggar a big boost with Gimbels, which had just bought the line in depth for the first time.

Haggar continued to forge a relationship with the athletic-minded consumer. It became a TV sponsor of sporting events, especially professional football. The company enjoyed title sponsorship of "This Week In The NFL" and produced spots for the Super Bowl. Athletes from Mickey Mantle to Roger Staubach appeared in ad endorsements.

In the 1970s, at a company sales meeting J.M. Haggar pulled Hite aside and said, "Morris, I just want to say that this company owes you a great deal for getting us on TV. I know I opposed it at the beginning. But when we started advertising on television was when we got out of the basement and started to get into the big time."

With potential print advertisers, Hite used a similar approach. When asked the cost of a a full-page, four-color ad in "Life" magazine, Hite replied, "Oh, about fifty grand I reckon."

"Fifty thousand dollars," they'd whistle. "That sure is a lot of money for *one ad*.

"Not for one ad," Hite corrected. "For six million ads."

(Six million was the circulation of Life, not an arbitrary number Morris had pulled out of the air.)

"That's enough ads to fill up this whole goddamn

room," Hite exclaimed. "Can you imagine that? It would take several trucks to haul them in here. LIFE prints the ad, surrounds it with the finest photos and writing and delivers it your home. It costs the advertiser *seven-tenths of one cent per ad.*

"That's less than a post card," Morris pointed out. "It's a real bargain, a *tremendous* bargain in mass selling."

But more than Hite's downhome charm or his uncanny salesmanship, advertisers kept their accounts with Hite and Tracy-Locke because he made them money. He helped their business *grow.*

In the early 1960s, Hite created a new product for Borden, called Hi-Pro milk. "Protein had become a fad word. Everyone was looking for a diet high in protein and low in fat. I got to thinking and thought 'Geez, milk is a hell of a source of protein.' I figured out how Borden could make a product with twice the protein and half the fat of regular milk if they increased the serum solids.

"I got together with Newt Lamb, the Borden lab guy in Houston, and we figured out that we could do it. How we could make the product and not let it taste like bluejohn (skim milk). Newt became real excited. He knew we had something.

"I did the dairy arithmetic and figured out they could produce the milk cheaper because it had a lower fat content. It would mean a difference of two cents on a half gallon if we sold it at the same price as regular homogenized milk. I named the product Hi-Pro and designed the packaging. The ad copy practically wrote itself: *Twice the protein and half the fat.*

Hite took his plan to the Borden people in Houston. Here's the product, he said. Here's how it's made, here's how we'll sell it, here's what we'll sell it for. Hite also recommended splitting the extra two cents in margin by taking one cent in profit and putting one cent in an accrual fund to build a sustaining ad budget for Hi-Pro.

"I sold the whole package except the advertising plan. Ben Putnam, who was the president of the division, said, "No, Morris, we'll take the whole two cents as profit. You already have an advertising budget. You'll have to use the advertising out of that."

"He'd have made more money if he'd followed my plan," Hite insisted. "The product never has been advertised adequately. It accounts for about 10 percent of Borden's milk sales and a higher percentage of profits but it could account for as much as 20 percent of volume.

"Ben wouldn't agree with that, even to this day," said Hite. "But I know different. . . ."

Hite passed the torch of product innovation to other account men at Tracy-Locke. "I think the thing that built this company has been innovative thinking," he maintained. "We have always tried to figure out a little different way to approach the problems than our competitors. That's become a tradition around here."

Tracy-Locke's innovation helped Frito-Lay crack a closed potato chip market in the Southwest, establishing an agency/client relationship that has flourished more than 30 years.

"When Frito Co. started to acquire Lay's potato chips, Frito wound up the one being acquired," Hite recalled. "Herman Lay moved to Dallas from Atlanta to take over the operation. Before that, Frito had very little to do with potato chips. I remember I'd go to a sales meeting, and someone in the back of the room would shout out 'Why don't we do something to sell some potato chips?' And the sales manager up at the podium would shout back, 'Just remember the name of this company is The Frito Co. and we sell Fritos.'

"Then Herman Lay came to town as boss and the

company's largest stockholder (he later became the largest shareholder of Frito-Lay parent Pepsico, Inc.) and he'd made his money in potato chips. He had no romantic attachment to Fritos.

"And the first thing he asked when he got to Dallas was 'Why the hell don't we sell some potato chips?'

"And the answer came back: 'That's a good question, why the hell don't we?'

"And then Mr. Lay came down to Tracy-Locke and asked me, 'Why the hell don't we sell some potato chips?'

"And I said to him, 'By God, I think we should.'"

Frito-Lay and Tracy-Locke found Lay's entry in the potato chip business in the Southwest blocked by Morton. Morton dominated the potato chip market much the same as Frito dominated corn chips. Morton's sales strategy consisted of keeping its grocery chain customers entertained. Morton spent little money on consumer advertising, but entertained grocers in grand style, providing tickets to The Masters, Indy 500, Kentucky Derby and other major sporting events. Morton relied on the old-boy network to ensure its business.

The absence of consumer advertising created a wedge for Tracy-Locke. "Our research showed that potato chip consumption in the Midwest was twice that in the Southwest," said Hite. "Potato chips are a volume item for a grocer and carry a good markup. We prepared individualized presentations for each of the major grocery chains. We went in and said 'You're selling so many dollars of potato chips. How would you like to sell *twice* that much?'

"That got their attention," Morris chuckled. "But really they were saying to themselves, 'Okay, how are you going to do that?'"

"And we said, 'Look, Morton's spending virtually nothing on advertising. We propose to sell potato chips directly to your customers. We'll bring customers into your store. We'll double your business.'"

To boost consumer trial of Lay's, Tracy-Locke created a sales promotion offering a $1 refund to people who mailed in the labels off three 49-cent bags. "We came up with a fresh idea," said Hite. "By now it's been beaten to death, but back then it was different." Especially since most coupons offered five or ten cents off—not a whole dollar.

"Suddenly the grocer said to himself, 'Goddamn, I better put in those Lay's potato chips because I know my customers will want to get those dollar bills.' And the whole time he's thinking to himself, 'I'll put in Lay's for this one promotion, then I'll throw these sons of a bitches out of my store and go back to Morton's.'"

The grocers had anticipated Tracy-Locke's promotional assault. "We hit them with promotion after promotion," said Hite. "Another and another. We promoted the hell out of Lay's potato chips and we forced our way into the stores. Everybody, all the major chains, put us in. Finally, Lay's flat ran Morton out of the market."

To support the Lay's introduction, Tracy-Locke created a broadcast campaign built around the slogan *So crisp you can hear their freshness.*

"It was a good line, but we didn't execute it well," said Hite. "We didn't have the imagination to present it in a dramatic enough way. All we did was use a pretty girl and crank up the sound when she bit into the chip.

"Anyway, Herman Lay came up to me after that and told me that our work on Lay's was the greatest introductory campaign he'd ever seen. And then goes ahead and hires Young & Rubicam to roll it out nationally . . ."

Frito-Lay had other plans in store for Tracy-Locke. In the mid-1960s, Tracy-Locke received the go-ahead to develop the Doritos brand tortilla chip. The acid test for the agency's role came when sales in test markets with no advertising support were compared with sales in test markets where Tracy-Locke bought spot TV. The ad-supported markets outsold the other markets two-to-one, validating the agency's effort.

Frito-Lay officials, impressed with the results, gave Tracy-Locke additional responsibility. The agency account service group, led by Stewart Mitchell, coordinated the expansion of Doritos into more test markets nationally. The brand quickly showed it had more than regional appeal. By 1966, Doritos had been rolled out nationally. Sales approached $10 million.

In 1968, Tracy-Locke introduced a line extension for Doritos, a taco-flavored version of the original chip. The agency's timetable called for a 12- to 18-month test period, but within seven months the new chip had been rolled out nationally.

Tracy-Locke introduced two other chips for Frito-Lay, Prontos and Funyuns. Both showed impressive speed out of the test gate, but each lacked the widespread appeal of Doritos, which had turned into a snack food monster.

By the time the Avery Schreiber TV commercials hit air in the late 1960s, Doritos had become a $50 million brand. Within two years, it topped the $100 million sales barrier. It was hailed in marketing circles as one of the best brand introductions of the 1960s.

Not to rest on its laurels, Tracy-Locke rolled out another product extension, called Nacho Cheese Doritos. The agency named the product, designed the package, worked with the R&D to perfect the taste. It became a huge success of its own in the 1980s, outstripping the original Doritos in annual sales.

Later in the 1970s, Tracy-Locke developed yet another new product for Frito-Lay: Tostitos. The agency built its creative strategy around finding the owner of a Mexican restaurant who could vouch for the authentic Mexican taste. But weeks of searching for a TV spokesman led nowhere. Finally, central casting sent over an actor named

Fernando Escandon. He looked and sounded right for the role. "Oh by the way," Fernando said, "I own a little restaurant out in the Valley."

Like Avery Schreiber before him, another star was born.

All of the agency's innovative thinking for Frito-Lay brought its own rewards: growth. Tracy-Locke not only picked up the $7 million Lay's budget in 1980, it gained entrée through Frito-Lay to Pepsico headquarters in Purchase, New York. The agency received several substantial assignments from Pepsico units, including the Pepsi Bottlers' Group nationwide and Taco Bell.

Another example of Morris Hite's philosophy of account service—the big idea—helped Tracy-Locke score a major success with the introduction of Dole bananas. The summer '72 introduction helped smooth out a rocky period for the agency.

Tracy-Locke had been working for Standard Fruit and Steamship out of New Orleans since the late 1950s. In 1967, the client decided to test market bananas under the Cabana name.

At the time, Castle and Cooke Foods, which marketed canned pineapples under the Dole label, had a working interest in Standard Fruit and Steamship. Tracy-Locke urged the client to capitalize on the Dole brand name rather than start from scratch with Cabana. Castle and Cooke quashed the idea. But several years later, the two companies merged. Don Kirchhoff, president of Standard Fruit, took over at Castle and Cooke. He liked the idea of using the Dole name.

Jim Killinger at the agency wrote the line "Dole Has Gone Bananas," which account man Willard Moon resurrected from the creative director's scrap bin. Willard Moon, who later opened Tracy-Locke's San Francisco office, helped fine-tune the media in the California test market, concentrating on Saturday morning kids shows and 3-week bursts rather than the scheduled 12-week plan.

Backed with strong point-of-sale materials and a classic premium item—an inflatable banana—Tracy-Locke helped Dole become the nation's best-selling banana within 18 months.

Castle and Cooke went bananas over Tracy-Locke's work, assigning the agency introduction of Dole fresh pineapples and fresh mushrooms. Just as Morris had always said, if you make money for your clients, they'll take care of you. Castle and Cooke pumped a $4 million ad budget into Tracy-Locke in the mid-1970s, ranking it third behind Frito-Lay and Phillips Petroleum.

The personal side of advertising relationships cannot be overplayed when discussing account service. Though not absolutely essential to success in the agency business, having people skills can help immeasurably.

Morris Hite developed lasting friendships with clients. Men like Ed Miller of Jones-Blair Paint, Ken Laird of Imperial Sugar, Ray Duvall and Lew Torrance of Borden were among Morris's closest friends. He'd hunt and fish with them, play golf and poker, swap jokes and lies.

He had their confidence and trust, something he earned over time by his approach to their business. He made the effort to help his clients, no matter what their problems, and they didn't forget.

"I've noticed in my career that most business is done on relationships," said Steve Hanna, a Tracy-Locke account man on Borden who ultimately left advertising for real estate. "Morris had a tremendous ability to develop close personal relationships in a very short period of time. He was able to maintain those relationships based on his experience and devotion to his clients' business."

Morris Hite liked people. The same aura that turned clients into friends endeared him to agency employees. He kept an open door policy. If you need to see Morris Hite about something, come on in. And he knew them all early by name. Even the most junior media buyer or copywriter might be surprised to hear Hite call out his name on the elevator.

Morris mastered the art of management through little touches. He refrained from humiliating, or putting down, employees. He could get a writer or art director to change creative direction without bruising egos. He could be loud and profane—and frequently was—but didn't direct his anger at people so much as bad ideas.

Despite his formidable presence, Morris Hite was a softie at heart. A softie who couldn't bring himself to fire employees, and with few exceptions delegated the deed. A softie who moved easily into the role of the agency's senior statesman, giving advice to young account people, taking time to speak to student groups whenever he was asked.

Stewart Mitchell, speaking to one such student ad group in the early 1970s, remarked, "One thing that won't change in the next 25 years of advertising is the concept of service . . . an advertising agency is a service business. Over the long haul, its success will depend solely on how well it serves the needs of its clients. An agency's size, rate of growth, profitability and the respect and recognition it commands within the industry may take the form of goals. But they are not ends in themselves. They are results. The results of superior service to clients."

"You must get involved and stay involved in your customer's business," urged Mitchell. "His business is your business. You should study his sales constantly, and his profits. Because these are the ultimate yardsticks by which your service will be measured."

Mitchell's mentor, Morris Hite, would have said the same thing.

CHAPTER SIXTEEN

"IF AN AD CAMPAIGN IS BUILT AROUND A WEAK IDEA—OR AS IS SO OFTEN THE CASE, NO IDEA AT ALL—I DON'T GIVE A DAMN HOW GOOD THE EXECUTION IS, IT'S GOING TO FAIL."—MORRIS HITE

In the summer of 1979, Morris Hite reprised parts of his Account Executive's Training School for the staff of Point Communications. Point, which Bill Neale opened in 1970 as Tracy-Locke's design studio, had expanded its scope beyond producing brochures, annual reports and collateral materials. Point had evolved into a full-service ad agency.

Mindful of that evolution and what it implied for account service, Neale wanted the Point staff to hear the ad gospel according to Hite. Especially Morris' thoughts on what constitutes good account service.

Hite accepted Neale's invitation with the caveat that the sessions number three instead of 13. The first meeting took place on June 20, 1979, at Point's office in the Metropolitan Savings building. Morris began by saying that although he hoped to give the Point staff some examples of effective ad campaigns and some insight into advertising strategies, he could only point to a trail of knowledge, not lead them down it.

"I can't teach you to be an advertising person in three weeks," Hite said. "Sometimes you can't teach someone to be an advertising person in a lifetime.

"You have to teach yourself. You can go to Harvard or

Stanford or anyplace else and they can't teach you to be an advertising person. You have do if for yourself. *You* have to be the one to read and study on your own."

Hite spent the first Point session tracing the history of Tracy-Locke, its evolution from the Southwestern Advertising Co. to Tracy-Locke-Dawson to Tracy-Locke Co. He repeated the story of how Shelley Tracy, Raymond Locke and Joe Dawson became known for their integrity by forgoing bankruptcy and repaying their debts. How Tracy-Locke-Dawson's New York office flourished while its Dallas office languished with one major account, Dr Pepper, until an inevitable clash occurred. How the agency's philosophy through the years had remained: *do whatever is necessary to help clients achieve profitable sales increases.*

"This business goes in spurts," said the 69-year-old Hite, reflecting on 42 years at Tracy-Locke. "When we handled the Maryland Club introduction and landed the Frito account, we reached one level. We hit another level with Pearl Beer. When we sold Frontier Airlines and Phillips we hit new plateaus."

He also touched on Tracy-Locke's diversification, especially its success in market research. "Last year ['78], MARC and Tracy-Locke were roughly the same size operation. The agency was more profitable, but each of them brought in about $12 million in revenues."

Morris reminded the group that the same diversification phase spawned Point Communications. "Bill [Neale] came to me in 1970 and said 'You know, last year we paid $150,000 to freelance artists and graphics designers. Maybe we should keep that business for ourselves.' He's shown there was money to be made off the guy who needs brochures or annual reports."

By 1979, Point's revenues had reached $1.2 million, or roughly those of an ad agency billing about $8 million. "I think there's a helluva opportunity out there for Point," said Morris. "There's a helluva need for second-tier agencies to serve intermediate accounts that don't require the expensive services of a larger agency like Tracy-Locke."

But even intermediate accounts require professional account service, which explained the point of the sessions.

SESSION TWO

In session two on June 27, Morris turned to his pet subject: ideas and idea-hunting. "There are not too many really good advertising ideas," he observed. "And the better the idea, the less time it takes to describe it.

"A good idea can be written in one or two sentences. It's the weak idea that takes page after page to try to sell. If you can't write your idea on one page, it's not that strong."

Hite chuckled. "It makes me think of what J.M Haggar of The Haggar Co. used to tell me when I went in to sell him an idea. He'd say, 'Don't romance me. Just tell me your idea and what it's going to cost me.'"

"Advertising is an idea business," Hite continued. "If you can build a campaign around a good idea, even if the execution is mediocre it may still be a successful campaign. But if a campaign is built around a weak idea—or so often is the case, no idea at all—I don't give a damn how good the execution is, the campaign is going to fail."

Morris drew a distinction between two types of advertising ideas—selling ideas or literary ideas. Hite shared a story he'd read in *Tested Advertising Methods*, a classic advertising book written by New York adman John Caples. ("It seems all the really good ad books," he sighed, "were written years ago.")

Caples had related the story of how Alexander Hamilton Institute in Brooklyn, seeking to enroll students in its mail-order business courses, had engaged a New York agency to write a direct solicitation ad. The agency's copywriter had penned a literary masterpiece that used as its headline a Biblical phrase, "The Years The Locust Hath

Eaten," and told a moving story about opportunities not realized.

"People in the advertising fraternity loved the ad," drawled Hite. "It was beautifully written, read like poetry almost. It won all kinds of awards and advertising people hailed it as a classic. Anyway, at the bottom of the ad was a coupon that people could send in to enroll in the course."

A subsequent ad for the Alexander Hamilton Institute took a different tack. This time the headline read "What A Young Man Must Know To Make $10,000 A Year," and the copy outlined the business courses included in the program.

"You have to consider that $10,000 dollars was a helluva lot of money in those days," said Hite. "If a guy could get to 10 grand a year he had it made. Anyway, this second ad received no acclaim from the ad industry. It was purely a nuts and bolts ad. But Caples, who was research director at BBDO, checked the numbers and found it out-pulled the 'Locust' ad by something like 30 or 40 to 1."

The story illustrated Hite's point that advertising messages should be persuasive, not profound.

"Lots of times in this business we get hung up with the way things are said. Writers especially think that a clever turn of phrase or a beautiful combination of words motivates people. But you have to remember the average guy you're trying to reach is a selfish sonofabitch who doesn't give a damn about literary gems. When you hit him with something like 'What A Young Man Must Know to Make $10,000 A Year,' you're appealing to his selfish interests."

"Advertising isn't out there to educate, or to make better people out of the masses," said Hite. "It's out there to sell. Some people may think that's bad, but if *you* think it's bad you shouldn't be in this business."

Literary ads, said Hite, face insurmountable odds. "The problem with ads that try to appeal on literary merit is that you're trying to compete with the news guy. And you're dead going in because he's got things to write about like murder, robbery, rape, incest, all those things people find fascinating. You're writing an ad about a product or a service. You don't have a chance."

"Some of you people in account service will never write an ad yourself. But the point is it's important to teach yourself whether an ad is good or not. Particularly for account executives, it would be fatal not to recognize a good idea going in."

Hite said an accomplished account executive should be well-rounded enough to generate all kinds of ideas—advertising, selling, product, research—for clients. "An advertising professional must be able to analyze sales and marketing problems and develop innovative solutions," Morris insisted.

"Let me give you an example," he said. "In 1954, I solicited and sold the southwest division of Frito Co. This was before it became Frito-Lay. At the time, Frito had complete market distribution and very small sales increases. The product (corn chips) received good shelf space and good exposure in the grocery store.

"The problem we faced was how the hell could we get them more sales? The normal way you do that in the food business is to get more distribution. Get the product in more stores with more shelf space. But Frito already had that. It was the only corn chip in the market.

"Our research showed us we should base our strategy on regular users. That we should try to get people already eating Fritos to eat more of them. We tried to convince them to use Fritos, which was a snack item, with other foods. With soups or salads or sandwiches. Or with a cold drink.

"We created sales growth for Frito by creating a campaign with the slogan 'Things taste better with Fritos.' It proved to be a very successful campaign. And ten years or so later, Coca-Cola did a great job with 'Things Go Better

With Coke.' They did a much better creative job than we did, but the idea was the same.

"But that's another thing about ideas," he noted. "It's interesting to see how ideas come along and are used. There's a campaign out now you've seen on TV that says 'Thanks, Paine Webber.' About five or six years ago we had a TV spot called 'Thanks, Haggar.' It was a situational spot done in a light vein where the guy gets the date because of his Haggar clothes. I'm sure the guy who wrote the Paine Webber spot doesn't think he copied it."

"Ideas are the guts of the ad business," said Hite. "If we really do our job well, we'll develop ideas to solve any kind of problem the client may have.

"I was talking to the guys at Tracy-Locke last night, telling them I wasn't so sure they haven't hired too many marketing guys instead of advertising guys. We got into a helluva an argument over a bottle of Johnny Walker Red.

"As I see it, an advertising person is a person who can develop ideas. A marketing guy can sit down with a calculator and get the cost of goods and the cost to sell it and subtract the selling price and so on, and come up with a gross profit. Then he figures with his calculator if total consumption is so much and if I can get 5 percent of the market the first year . . . punch, punch, punch . . . then I can make so much money. And then he subtracts out the cost of advertising . . . punch, punch, punch . . . and if he hasn't got anything left (pause) then he changes the goddamn numbers. And he says to himself, 'Geez, I better get 6 percent.' And then he punches out those numbers.

"Now this is an essential part of the business, figuring out a marketing plan. But how the hell are you going to make that happen? Who's the guy who's going to go out and get that 6 percent?

"Most of our clients have people who can punch this stuff out on the calculator. I say what they need are the people who can get them that 6 percent. With advertising ideas and sales ideas and packaging ideas. They need people who generate ideas. Adpeople."

Adpeople like Hite, anyway.

Morris said many of his good ideas germinated from thinking he'd done behind the wheel of his car. "When you're driving home in the evening, you'll have plenty of time to go over a problem in your mind. Turn it over and over. Then the next day, when you're not even thinking about the problem, something will pop into your head.

"It's a funny thing, the human mind," he said. "We don't really know where ideas comes from. But I do know the more you worry the problem in your head, going over it again and again, the better chance you have of coming up with a solution."

Hite urged the Point staffers to discipline themselves to be students of advertising. He'd given the same advice to Tracy-Locke's account men two decades earlier. "Study other ads, even in unrelated product fields. Look at every ad and ask yourself what is it trying to tell me? What's the idea back of this ad? What's the strategy?

"Too many times you'll say to yourself, 'Jesus Christ, all they're trying to do is fill up the goddamn space.' That's because they don't have anything to say. But when you see good ads, you'll quickly see what they're talking about."

Morris also suggested that adpeople should pay particular attention to TV commercials because television represented "the greatest advertising medium we've ever had."

"I don't watch TV programs myself," he said. "I can't stand most of that crap on the air. But when the commercials come on, I'll put down the book I'm reading and watch. Because that's not entertainment, that's my business. I watch and study commercials, and I ask myself two questions: 'Did I get a solid reason to buy this product?' and 'Do I have a good feeling about the product?'"

In conclusion, Hite burst the bubble of anyone who

believed in advertising short-cuts. Good ideas, he suggested, came from probing into a product and refusing to settle for the first idea that popped into mind.

"There's no secret formula for advertising success," said Morris, "other than to learn everything you can about the product. Most products have some unique characteristic, and the really great advertising comes right out of the product and says something about the product that no one else can say. Or at least no one else *is* saying."

SESSION THREE

As a practical exercise for session three on July 3, 1979, Bill Neale divided the Point staffers into three teams, which were told to select their favorite ongoing ad campaign and analyze its intent and effectiveness. Morris Hite, as professor emeritus, would then critique each of the presentations.

Team One picked a TV campaign for Oscar-Mayer bologna. Team Two chose a multimedia campaign for the Bell Telephone System. Team Three tapped a print campaign for Chivas Regal.

"I agree that Oscar-Mayer is an excellent campaign," said Hite. "Oscar-Mayer has been one of the most effective advertisers over the past 10 or 20 years. They've been able to establish a brand name and a reputation for quality. They've convinced the public it's worth the extra few cents you pay for a premium brand.

"They've bowed their necks and closed their eyes and made the decision to penetrate the sonic barrier of indifference. You've got to cut through that barrier if you're going to make your advertising pay off."

Hite also praised Oscar-Mayer for its use of jingles. "Jingles are a very effective way to sell kid's products, which bologna is. Kids are susceptible to jingles. You just have to remember in writing a jingle to make sure everyone can understand the brand name. We've done a few jingles at Tracy-Locke where you couldn't tell what goddamn product was being sold."

The use of jingles reminded Hite of one of his tenets of broadcast advertising, which he shared with the group: "If you don't have anything to say, sing it."

After hearing the Bell Telephone presentation, Hite offered several thoughts. He especially liked the casting of character actor Ed Andrews as spokesman. "I think he does a remarkable job. He adds just enough comedic touch to the spots, yet he's not such a buffoon that he detracts from the credibility and believability of the spot.

"There's a fine line in TV advertising," Morris observed. "If you get too damn funny you can overpower the message. Sometimes with humor you find people know the spots but they don't know who the advertiser is or what the hell is being sold. You've got to make sure the humor doesn't get in the way of the selling message."

Another of Hite's advertising tenets, which he didn't share on that particular day, concerns the use of humor: "When you're trying to write that funny commercial, just remember its h-a-a-a-r-d to make a client laugh."

The Bell campaign, which included the award-winning "Reach Out and Touch Someone" series of spots, makes a strong emotional touch with its audience, said Hite, "and these types of campaigns can create a lot of goodwill for the advertiser."

The Chivas Regal presentation centered around a holiday season gift campaign that appeared in upscale business and consumer magazines like *Fortune, Forbes* and *Esquire.*

"This is the work of Doyle Dane Bernbach," said Morris. "It shows a high degree of creativity around a pretty dull subject, a bottle of booze. But they've created a classic campaign, where they feature the product and really establish an image as a 'Tiffany' brand of Scotch.

"We always said that the biggest cliché in this business is to show a picture of the factory. If you need an ad approved in a hurry, make a quick layout that features the factory or the product. If we ever got into a bind on Mrs Baird's we used to come up with a layout where seven-eighths of it showed a loaf of bread. The Bairds thought that was the most beautiful thing they'd ever seen. We knew they'd approve it."

"The Chivas campaign started back in the 1960s, about the time Doyle Dane also did the Volkswagen work. It's easy to look at this and see it's great work. But it's not always easy to tell a good idea when you're looking at something in rough tissue form. You can make some bad mistakes.

"I've been guilty of turning down some good ideas," Morris admitted. "Back when we had Pearl Beer and were using the "Country of 1,100 Springs," theme, Bill Mitchell came up with the line 'You can take Pearl out of the country, but you can't take the country out of Pearl."

"I turned it down. And damned if Salem cigarettes didn't come along a few years later and have a great success with "You can take Salem out of the country, but you can't take the country out of Salem."

(Hite, being Hite, would freely admit his mistakes. Point account man Willard Moon recalled receiving a phone call in the early 1970s from a friend at a California agency who had heard Morris speak at a western region ad conference.

"I can't believe your boss," said the caller. "He actually stood up there and said the agency had done some things wrong. I've never heard an adman that candid."

"That's Morris, all right," Moon replied.)

Mitchell's line wasn't the only big idea Hite blew for Pearl. "I also turned down a wonderful line Alan Meyer wrote, 'Pearl: It's The Real Thing.' You probably heard of it. Coca-Cola used it later and had a major success."

Morris praised the durability of the Chivas campaign. "It can be difficult keeping a campaign going. First you have to keep the client sold on the idea, and then you have to keep the campaign fresh by making the little modifications that keep consumers interested enough to want to continue to look, listen and read."

Nevertheless, Hite ventured the guess that the biggest waste of money in advertising results from unnecessary changes. "I learned that lesson years ago," he said. "I had a friend who was a cub writer on the *Daily Oklahoman*. Mr. E.K. Gaylord, one of the all-time great publishers in the Southwest, owned the paper and he personally approved every editorial on the editorial page. As you might guess, he was very conservative.

"My friend's job was to go into Mr. Gaylord's office every morning at 7:30 and listen to the old man harangue on this or that subject. The kid would take notes and then draft up an editorial based on whatever Mr. Gaylord had said. Gaylord was a talker, not a writer.

"Anyway, one time Mr. Gaylord got off on an upcoming bond election. Every day he'd have something new to say about the bond election, which he favored. After two months of writing about the same bond every day, my friend finally blurted out, "Mr. Gaylord, I've written so many editorials on this issue already that I believe if I have to write one more word about it, I'll throw up on my typewriter.'

"And Mr. Gaylord look at him and said, 'Young Man, when you've written so many editorials that you actually *do* throw up on your typewriter, then we might just assume that the public is barely becoming aware of what we're trying to say.'

"That's something I've never forgotten," said Morris. "But what happens in advertising is that the client first sees the ad in rough form. And when it's finished, he sticks it on the wall. He shows it to his wife and she comments on it. So do his friends. Pretty soon he's tired of it.

"But chances are that when the client's already sick

and tired of it, the marketplace is only about 20 percent aware that he's even running the goddamn thing.

"There's no question," observed Morris, "that there's too much bland advertising that nobody even knows is being run. Except for the client who paid for it and the people at the agency, particularly the creatives, who created it."

Hite concluded the training sessions by fielding questions from the Point staff. Several asked about the entertainment value of commercials. Hite showed his true colors by responding:

"I don't totally buy the argument that commercials have to entertain. The number one job is to build brand identification and to sell.

"Now if you can figure out how to do that—build brand ID and sell—in an entertaining way, then you have the possibility of creating a memorable piece of advertising. But, and I'm repeating myself here, there's a fine line you've got to be careful not to cross. You can't let the entertainment overpower the message or interfere with the sale. Entertainment should support the selling message, not smother it."

Any more questions? OK, students, class dismissed.

CHAPTER SEVENTEEN

"WE'VE GOT A LOT OF MONEY COMING THROUGH THIS PLACE—BUT THERE AIN'T ENOUGH STICKING TO THE WALLS."—MORRIS HITE

Tracy-Locke's billings shot over the $100 million mark in 1979 and by the beginning of the 1980s, the agency began looking at itself with a national rather than regional perspective. After its dramatic success with Frito-Lay, especially developing Doritos and Nacho Cheese Doritos and rolling out Tostitos, the agency assumed a new assertiveness. Call it a (snack) chip on the shoulder.

But two separate incidents gave the agency's principals pause. In the late 1970s, Tracy-Locke unsuccessfully pitched for the blue-chip account of Pizza Hut. Agency executives believed they'd made their best possible bid for the business, and felt good about their chances for winning the account up to the moment they received word that Foote, Cone & Belding had been the pizza chain's choice.

The bottom-line seemed to be size. Foote Cone billed more than $1 billion annually—ten times the volume of Tracy-Locke. Its field staff in place to service the needs of Pizza Hut franchises was infinitely wider and deeper. As much as anything else, Tracy-Locke had been outnetworked.

The Dallas agency began a critical period of self-examination. Less and less did it compete against regional-type agencies for regional-type accounts. Bidding for national accounts meant facing competition from national every time out. There's a price to be paid for success.

Internally, Tracy-Locke began a critical self-examination to see if it had the infrastructure—the right people and right mix of skills—to be competitive on a national level. Norm Campbell, Stewart Mitchell and other senior executives also began to ponder avenues to ensure future growth.

Conversations tended to focus on three possible scenarios:

- Should Tracy-Locke remain a strong independent, buying some smaller shops to reinforce its status as a major "Sunbelt" agency?
- Should Tracy-Locke find another agency in the $100 million to $300 million range with which to merge?
- Should Tracy-Locke hook up with one of the mega-agencies in the U.S., a shop doing business worldwide?

The consensus view, with some dissenting opinions, was that the first two options would limit Tracy-Locke's growth over the next 10 to 15 years and that for the foreseeable future in advertising, big shops would get bigger. Size was where it's at.

While debate ensued internally, a second external event influenced management's thinking. In September 1980, Texas Instruments moved its account from Tracy-Locke to McCann-Erickson. The TI loss proved to be a portent, however, because it underscored for Norm Campbell and his cohorts the need for Tracy-Locke to have an international capability—either directly or through an affiliate arrangement. TI had moved to McCann in part because of the agency's affiliation with The Interpublic Cos., a worldwide network.

Ringing in Campbell's ears were the words of TI boss Mark Sheperd, who said that if he slammed his desk in Dallas he wanted the reverberations to be felt around the world. Sheperd's comment reflected the global view of multinational marketers, big-picture people who wished to do business with big-picture ad agencies.

So Norm Campbell, who once joked that he planned to turn over the reins to Tracy-Locke when it reached $100 million in billings—a statement his associates pointed out when the agency crossed the threshold—turned his attention to a new front: mergers and acquisitions.

The ad industry presented no shortage of case studies to analyze. Like virtually every other established U.S. industry, advertising had undergone a substantial consolidation in the post-World War II economy. Major New York and Chicago agencies had spread their tentacles across the United States, enveloping local agencies from St. Louis to Seattle. Growth markets on the West Coast like Los Angeles and San Francisco proved particularly popular.

Cannibalization of local and regional ad agencies generally proved to be more successful than colonization, since the Manhattan method of doing business didn't always work well west of the Hudson River. Some national shops learned the hard way about the advantages of giving a local shop a new name but keeping its management in place.

In the mid-1970s, Tracy-Locke provided a prime prospect for national agencies. Morris Hite's outfit had everything you look for in an acquisition target, and more:

- Headquarters in the Sunbelt, the nation's prime growth market.
- A blue-chip account list, headed by Frito-Lay, a major packaged-goods player.
- An experienced management group headed by Hite and Campbell.
- A strong balance sheet.

But Tracy-Locke spurned several suitors. Though Hite frequently said he'd never turn down the chance to talk with another agency, because "every time you talk to these people you learn something you didn't already know," no one ever made Morris an offer he couldn't refuse.

Tracy-Locke remained independent throughout the 1970s. So did another of Dallas' three large shops, The Bloom Agency, operated by agency founder Sam Bloom and his son, Bob. Only Glenn Advertising opted to sell out, being merged into Bozell & Jacobs in 1974.

In Houston, by contrast, national agencies made inroads as early as the 1950s. In 1953, McCann-Erickson acquired Wilkinson, Schiwetz & Tips, which handled the Humble Oil account. (Agency principal Kern Tips had already become a regional celebrity for his broadcasts of Southwest Conference football games on the Humble radio network.) Later, Foote Cone & Belding entered Houston by buying out Wilhelm, Laughlin & Wilson. Young & Rubicam acquired Rives Dyke.

Tracy-Locke in the mid-1970s had conducted conversations of varying scope and intensity with many of the largest U.S. ad agencies, shops like J. Walter Thompson, Foote, Cone & Belding, Ted Bates, Doyle Dane Bernbach and Young & Rubicam. The most serious suitor proved to be Foote, Cone & Belding. By 1978, Norm Campbell took part in an extended series of conversations with top FC&B executives, which escalated to the point that Campbell spent a week touring all of the New York agency's domestic offices.

Morris Hite stayed in the background during the negotiations. He had authorized Campbell to negotiate any deal he deemed suitable, as long as it involved a stock swap or considerations other than cash. Tax purposes, you understand.

Campbell came close to cutting a deal with Foote, Cone & Belding. Morris and Tom Forman accompanied Norm to New York to negotiate an agreement but at the eleventh hour Campbell changed his mind and called a halt to the proceedings.

The trio flew back to Dallas and spent the afternoon on the golf course. Later, they adjourned to the Campbell's house, where Bob Brown and Stewart Mitchell joined them for a party. The admen broke out champagne and Johnny Walker scotch and toasted their independence.

Morris told Norm: "It was your call to make all the way. I'm just glad you did what you did." Tracy-Locke hadn't been ready to take on a new identity.

But by the spring of 1981, Tracy-Locke had begun looking in earnest for a merger partner. Howard Davis, one of the agency's senior vice presidents, and David Hudnall, secretary-treasurer, assisted Campbell in developing a list of criteria for ranking potential Tracy-Locke targets as parent companies. Their checklist, applied to the top ten U.S. agencies, encompassed the following areas:

- A good earnings record, indicative of management that knew how to make money.
- A strong reputation in creativity, which might create a halo effect on Tracy-Locke's own creative.
- An operating philosophy that gave autonomy to subsidiary companies.
- Strong international advertising capabilities.
- Account lists where few client conflicts would arise.
- Good "chemistry" between agency principals.

Davis and Hudnall's evaluation produced a short list of agencies to approach about a deal. At the top of the list: BBDO International, then the industry's sixth largest shop with worldwide billings of $1.3 billion.

BBDO International's core agency, BBDO, handled the Pepsi-Cola account. Because Pepsi's parent company, Pepsico, Inc., also owned Frito-Lay, account men from Tracy-Locke and BBDO occasionally met and interacted at Pepsico headquarters. The Pepsico tie-in created both an awareness level and comfort zone between BBDO and Tracy-Locke.

Ironically, BBDO had been the Madison Avenue shop

at which Norm Campbell had worked in the early 1960s before Tracy-Locke. Maybe you *can* go home again, Campbell thought to himself.

Placed against the globe, the prospective match seemed propitious. Tracy-Locke filled some gaps in U.S. operations for BBDO, which had a concentrated presence east of the Mississippi River. Internationally, BBDO's network of agencies from Europe to Asia extended Tracy-Locke's reach in every direction.

Moreover, Tracy-Locke's 1980 billings of $122 million represented a substantial enough proportion of BBDO's domestic operations (approx. $600 million) to ensure the Dallas agency would not be coming in as a small-time, second-string player.

Conversations between Norm Campbell and BBDO bosses Bruce Crawford and Allan Rosenshine began in the spring of 1981. They met in New York, in Dallas and at industry gatherings. Both sides would say later that from the outset of their talks, philosophies and chemistries clicked.

With merger plans afoot at Tracy-Locke, Morris Hite continued to oversee the Tracy-Locke Co. empire, which grew in various directions in the late 1970s. The agency's newest money-making avenue became real estate.

With the agency straining the seams of its space in the Metropolitan Savings building downtown, the Tracy-Locke board in 1976 approved the purchase of the Hartford building on the Dallas business district's long-neglected northeast side. The agency planned to occupy whatever space it needed for operations and lease the remainder of the 15-story building.

But by the time the agency got ready to move in 1979, demand for real estate in downtown Dallas had reached record levels. Foreign buyers representing Canadian, Japanese and Middle East interests had started a land rush in

Dallas, bidding up prices on commercial property. Even with the skyline dotted with building cranes, bringing more grade 'A' commercial space into the market, prices kept escalating.

So rather than move into the Hartford Building, Tracy-Locke elected to sell the property in the summer of 1979. The transaction netted the company $1.5 million after taxes. For its new corporate offices, Tracy-Locke leased space on four floors (approx. 70,000 sq. ft.) in the new Plaza of the Americas Tower, located three blocks east of the Hartford Building on Bryan Avenue. The agency moved into its new home in June 1980.

Morris Hite loved the view from his 32nd-floor office. "I can see the old Majestic Theatre building, where we worked when I came to Tracy-Locke in 1937," he said. "We were about 25 strong. I shared a small inside office with a girl copywriter. She was secretly in love with our vice president.

"I can also see our old building on Central Expressway. Making the decision to build was the first of several moves that gave our company new shape and substance. I liked my office there more than any I've ever had. Maybe it was because we owned the building."

Hite could admire and enjoy Tracy-Locke's handsomely appointed new offices, but he knew successful agencies had to be sharp, not look sharp. "These are the most sumptuous quarters we've ever occupied. The future of this agency never looked brighter. But handsome quarters alone will not make it shine. Doyle Dane Bernbach did its greatest work when headquartered in the garment district of New York. Steam pipes ran through their executive offices."

By 1980, Tracy-Locke Co. had made several real estate transactions, buying 17 acres in North Dallas nominally intended for a new headquarters building for M/A/R/C and 6.5 acres of land off Empire Central in the Stemmons

Freeway corridor of Northwest Dallas. Both investments brought sizable returns on investment to the agency. Sizable enough that Morris Hite, in an appearance before a group of advertising executives in '81, responded to a question about what he might do differently in his ad career by quipping, "I'd forget about advertising and go into real estate."

Tracy-Locke, M/A/R/C, Point, PSI—virtually every facet of Hite's "total communications company" proved to be a success, except for the still-photography operation, renamed Chromatek. It never produced the anticipated revenues and proved to be a drain on the profits. Tracy-Locke sold the company in 1981.

On November 19, 1980, four days ahead of the actual event, Morris Hite's associates at Tracy-Locke Co. honored him with a 70th birthday party. They made sure Morris got into the spirit of the occasion, hiring a belly-dancer to deliver a special birthday message. Ever the good sport, Morris tapped out time on a tambourine, covered his head with the dancer's veil and engaged in some old-fashioned bumping and grinding.

Hite's extended family at the agency gave him several gifts and mementos in a celebration that stretched over four floors and three hours. One of his most prized gifts came in the form of a poster called "The Sayings of Chairman Morris," a joint effort among Tracy-Locke, Point and M/A/R/C.

The poster included such Hite expressions as "Let me tell you boys, we'll be in deep shit when we start believing that the most important thing in this business is knowing how to read a Neilsen report" and "If we are going to make the deadline, we better quit fingering our clubs and get to writing some ads." (Morris, at Mrs. Hite's bidding, later edited the original X-rated poster into a PG-13 version suitable for framing.)

Dallas TV newscaster Chip Moody dropped in on the

birthday party to extend his best wishes to Morris, confessing he mistakenly thought he'd been invited to a retirement celebration. "Nah," corrected Morris, "they gave me a retirement party five years ago on my 65th birthday. Only I didn't get the hint."

Earlier in 1980, Morris Hite had been honored with the Horatio Alger Award, given annually to men and women who overcome humble beginnings to emerge as leaders in their respective fields. Hite received the award from Dr. Norman Vincent Peale, a fellow positive thinker, at a black-tie dinner in Detroit on May 16. One of Morris' longtime Dallas friends, W.W. "Foots" Clements, the CEO at Dr Pepper Co., also received one of the dozen awards presented that year.

For Hite and the other recipients, The Horatio Alger award represented the fulfillment of the American dream. Morris believed deeply in a free enterprise system that gave men and women the opportunity to succeed on their own terms.

Morris Hite at age 70 had only one thing sticking in his craw: the Borden Co. account. A management shakeup at Borden in 1979 resulted in a new group of managers taking over the dairy business in Houston. Borden executives who'd grown up in the company, working their way up from being the route man with a delivery trucks to the local plant manager to a job at division headquarters, suddenly found themselves being replaced by professional managers from outside the dairy industry.

Never mind that the bean-counters didn't know beans about milk or ice cream, they took over the top slots at Borden. They began to centralize operations at the division level, relieving local plant and sales managers of much of their autonomy. Morris openly and vocally criticized the new structure, arguing that the milk business depended on local alliances between sellers and suppliers. According to Hite, Borden's strength in the marketplace could be traced to the individuals who ran the local operations. Taking away their initiative and decision-making latitude and replacing it with a centralized management would be ruinous for business, argued Hite.

Tracy-Locke received the heave-ho shortly thereafter. Borden hired the flamboyant Jerry Della Femina to take over its account and Morris took the loss hard. He'd been working on the account since 1937. Some of his closest personal friends, like Ray Duvall, Lew Torrance, Wayne Moseley and John DeMouche were Borden executives.

By the summer of 1981, Tracy-Locke had worked out the details of its merger-to-be with BBDO International. Norm Campbell and Bruce Crawford had agreed in principle that BBDO would acquire Tracy-Locke Advertising and Public Relations, subject to the approval of each company's board of directors.

The other core elements of Tracy-Locke Co. would not be part of the deal. Since M/A/R/C enjoyed a close working relationship with Coca-Cola, Pepsi's arch-rival, the marketing research company never seriously figured in the merger plans. M/A/R/C, along with Point Communications, PSI and the other units would be combined in a holding company called Allcom (short for "All Communications"). Morris Hite would become chairman/CEO and Bud Phillips president and chief operating officer of the new company.

During the fall of 1981, while the lawyers and auditors ironed out the financial terms of Tracy-Locke's pending merger into BBDO International, Morris Hite received the news he'd been waiting several months to hear: that Borden had reversed its course and rehired Tracy-Locke as its ad agency.

Hite had been involved that summer in a letter-writing campaign to Borden executives at corporate headquarters in Columbus, Ohio, reminding them how much experience and expertise Tracy-Locke had with the dairy business. When the bean counters from outside the Borden ranks failed abjectly in Houston and some old dairy hands resumed control, Morris accompanied Tracy-Locke's Steve Hanna to an August meeting with the new dairy division president, Robert Kirby. Six weeks later, Kirby brought Tracy-Locke back on Borden.

Morris and his secretary, Suzi Reno, had to work overtime to answer all the correspondence he received from the Borden Co. ranks. A letter from a Jim Gravés in Amarillo summed up the prevailing sentiment: "Dear Morris," it read, "We received the good news of Tracy-Locke's return with Borden this week. We are all rejoicing over this."

Not pleased. Not happy. Not ecstatic. *Rejoicing*. Hite had that kind of effect on Borden personnel.

On February 1, 1982, Tracy-Locke completed its merger into BBDO International and changed its name to Tracy-Locke/BBDO, to indicate its new affiliation. Norm Campbell joined the New York agency's board of directors.

Tracy-Locke stockholders, 223 strong, received 52 percent of a BBDO share for each share of Tracy-Locke Co. stock they held, as well as one full share in Allcom, Inc. Morris Hite, who held roughly 110,000 shares of Tracy-Locke stock, received 53,000 shares in BBDO International. With a market value of roughly $40 a share, Hite's holdings eclipsed $2 million.

Morris moved out of Plaza of the Americas and set up shop next to Bud Phillips at M/A/R/C. Hite had plenty to occupy himself, including giving an assist to Andy Stern in the formation of Sunwest Communications, a public relations company that joined Allcom. Hite agreed with Stern, an ex-White House staffer, that a niche existed for counseling to senior management on communications strategies. It was the type of advice Hite gave his friends all the time for free; let Stern charge for the service.

By the summer of 1982, Morris turned his attention

back to his avocation: civic affairs. Dallas Mayor Jack Evans tapped Hite as chairman for a Dallas bond campaign that included 11 propositions totaling a record $247 million in planned improvements.

Hite welcomed the challenge. He well remembered the "Crossroads" campaign back in 1967. In fact, he remembered it so well he reprised parts of the ad series about the plight of Jefferson, Texas. The message had proved so effective in 1967—why not try it again?

Morris took his typically high-profile role in the '82 bond election, speaking to three or four civic groups a day and appearing on a carousel of TV, radio and newspaper forums. Hite, at 71, stood up to the rigors of the job as well as someone 20 years his junior.

Morris' game plan for the bond election was simple and direct. "Dallas: Yes" became the slogan. The propositions ranged from quality-of-life issues like the zoo ($18 million), city parks ($13 million), and a new concert hall ($29 million) to nitty-gritty municipal issues like flood control ($26 million) fire protection ($12 million) and street repairs ($105 million). As a whole they would make Dallas a better city in which to live, said Hite, and that would spur growth.

"The real key to successful marketing—I don't care whether you're selling a snack product or a suit of clothes—is to develop the product to where it serves the consumers' needs and can be delivered at a fair price," said Hite on election eve.

On Aug. 3, 1982, an unexpectedly high turnout approved all 11 propositions on the ballot. The smallest margin had been a 57.5 percent approval for a new symphony hall in the arts district.

Said Charles Anderson, city manager, "It's going to help everything, including our triple A bond rating, and it will ensure the quality of life in our city for the next 20 years."

Said Sid Stahl, city councilman, "It's a tremendous credit to the people of Dallas at a time when the economy is bad and property taxes are going up that they would give this vote of confidence to the city."

Said a *Dallas Morning News* editorial: "The fact that voters turned out in unexpectedly large numbers to approve all of the 11 propositions was testament, first, that the proposals were sound and, second, that Morris Hite did a mighty fine job."

No surprise there.

CHAPTER EIGHTEEN

"IMPROVE YOUR LIE? HELL, YES. THIS GAME IS HARD ENOUGH EVEN WHEN YOU CHEAT."
—MORRIS HITE

In September 1982, with the resoundingly successful Dallas bond campaign only a month behind him, Morris Hite took over as president of the Salesmanship Club of Dallas. Comprised of 600 businessmen from various professional groups, not necessarily sales, the Salesmanship Club ranked as Dallas' most powerful and prestigious civic organization.

Admission to the male-only club followed a screening process that carefully checked a candidate's record as a community leader, fundraiser, church member and civic volunteer. Three out of four wasn't enough. Upon admission to the Salesmanship Club a new member learned what was expected of him: attend a weekly Thursday luncheon and agree to devote substantial amounts of time and money to the club's activities.

A group of Dallas businessmen formed the Salesmanship Club in 1920 to provide a summer camp for indigent youths. The founding members acquired the property for the camp site and erected a facility in a matter of days, establishing a "can-do" spirit that subsequently became the club's byword.

By 1987, the Salesmanship Club's service program supported year-round boys' and girls' camps for troubled youth ages 11 to 16 and a family education and counseling center in Dallas. To generate operating funds, the Salesmanship Club drew on two revenue sources: a Dallas Cowboys' pre-season football game each August and the Byron Nelson Golf Classic each May.

In 1967, the Salesmanship Club sponsored the final Greater Dallas Open played at Oak Cliff Country Club in South Dallas. The following year it moved the event to Preston Trail Golf Club in North Dallas and renamed the tournament the Byron Nelson Golf Classic.

Byron Nelson had made his home in the area since the mid-1940s, when he semi-retired from professional golf to his Fairway Oaks ranch in Roanoke, Texas, not far from the DFW Airport. The Dallas tournament (renamed the GTE Byron Nelson Classic in 1988) thus became the first and only PGA Tour event named in honor of a professional player.

By then, the Salesmanship Club also had a strong affiliation with the Dallas Cowboys. In the team's infancy in the early 1960s, general manager Tex Schramm had designated that proceeds from the first home exhibition game each season would go to the Salesmanship Club's youth program. By the mid-1960s, when Tom Landry had fashioned Dallas into a championship contender, the Salesmanship Club game against Green Bay became the hottest sports ticket in town.

In 1981, Morris Hite served as chairman of the Byron Nelson Golf Classic, which for several reasons turned out to be among the most dramatic in the tournament's history. Tom Watson, a protege of Byron Nelson who had won in Dallas in 1978, 1979 and again in 1980, came in gunning for a fourth consecutive win.

As tournament chairman, Morris played in the featured pairing of the Wednesday pro-am with the defending champion. In addition to Hite and Watson, the featured fivesome included Dallas businessmen Paul Thayer and Ed Haggar (Morris' ad client) and comedian Bob Hope.

Hope had to duck out after 9 holes that day, saying "thanks for the memories" and racing to catch a plane.

Shortly after starting the back nine with Hope—Morris played most of his golf without hope—the group heard a roar from the gallery on the front nine.

"That's a hole in one," observed Watson.

"How do you know?" asked Hite.

Elementary, my dear Morris, replied Watson: "It sounds different from anything else we hear out here."

Sure enough, Dallas Cowboys coach Tom Landry had aced the 8th hole, sinking a four-iron shot from 165 yards.

When the tournament proper began, Watson delighted the Dallas galleries by tying for the first-round lead with a 64. In hot pursuit came a host of players, including Bruce Lietzke, who shot an opening 68 but grumbled, "I'm really not in love with Preston Trail. I don't have a lot of fun playing this golf course. It's not in very good shape."

Lietzke's criticism was the talk of the tournament until Friday morning. A severe storm, complete with high winds, lightning and rain, swept through Dallas, delaying play in the Nelson Classic. Shortly after the tournament resumed, a large tree limb suddenly snapped and fell, striking several spectators. One, a Bendix Corp. engineer who had driven down from Kansas City with three co-workers to watch the Nelson Classic, was killed, and a second person had to to be hospitalized.

"We have to assume the tree was damaged by the storm, but we don't know for sure," said the shaken tournament chairman. Hite later that day visited the injured spectator in her hospital room.

Watson returned things to normal on Saturday, staking a one-shot lead going into the final round. A record gallery turned out on Sunday to see him sew up his fourth straight win. But Watson stumbled to a 73 and had to sink a 15-foot birdie putt on the final hole to tie none other than Bruce Lietzke.

Watson seemed a solid bet in the sudden-death

play-off, and his birdie putt on the first playoff hole touched the cup before spinning out. Then to the disbelief of the Dallas fans, not to mention Byron Nelson, Watson missed his three-foot putt for par. Lietzke promptly tapped in to win the tournament.

At the awards ceremony that followed, Morris Hite congratulated the winner and handed him the $54,000 first-prize check. Noting Lietzke's criticism during the tournament, Morris drawled, "Hell, Bruce, what do reckon you could have shot if you *liked* this place?"

Morris Hite served another critical role for the tournament in late 1982. Working behind the scenes with Mike Massad, the tournament's ombudsman and liaison with the PGA Tour, Morris met with network TV officials to ensure that the Byron Nelson Classic would be telecast nationally.

ABC-TV, for which Byron Nelson had worked as a golf analyst, televised the Dallas tournament in the 1970s but dropped its option in 1979. In 1980 and 1981, NBC-TV picked up the TV rights, but in 1982 the Nelson Classic again found itself off the air.

Hite and Massad stepped in. They met in New York with executives of CBS Sports, which broadcast the Colonial National Invitation Tournament in Fort Worth the week preceding the Byron Nelson Classic. The Dallas duo pointed out that redeploying equipment and personnel the following week to Dallas, only 30 miles away, would mean few logistical worries and substantial cost savings.

Hite and Massad wanted Dallas to have national exposure and the Salesmanship Club to share in the revenues generated by network TV coverage. The Byron Nelson Classic already contributed more money to charity than any other PGA event. The Salesmanship Club took justifiable pride in that, and needed TV revenue to boost the tournament's bottom line.

A green light from the network (the PGA Tour held the ultimate approval) hinged on the issue of television sponsorship. Hite and Massad assured the CBS advertising sales executives they could line up commitments from TV sponsors.

The resulting sales effort reflected a cooperative spirit. Whoever could help, did. Rodger Meier, a Dallas Cadillac dealer, lined up sponsorship from American Airlines. Massad, an insurance man, brought in Equitable Life Insurance. (Equitable had participated in the development of Las Colinas in Irving, Texas, scheduled to become the tournament's new home in 1983.)

Morris Hite, together with Norm Campbell, secured a commitment from Frito-Lay. "Golf telecasts have fairly poor ratings and the audience obviously didn't fit with our target demographic," explained Frito-Lay executive Bill Korn, "but, frankly, we wanted to support the city of Dallas and support the Salesmanship Club's program. Several key clients went to bat and banded together to make certain the Nelson Classic didn't go off the air."

With the sponsorship assured and approval forthcoming from PGA Commissioner Deane Beman, the Salesmanship Club members looked forward to the 1983 tournament being back on national television.

In the spring of 1983, Morris and Caroline Hite spent more and more time at their home at the exclusive Lakeway resort near Austin, Texas. The Hites had finished building a second home there in 1980. Several Dallas friends bought condos and townhouses nearby, and the Hite's residence, the jacuzzi in particular, served as a gathering spot for the Dallas crowd.

Morris enjoyed getting away to Lakeway. He enjoyed being near two of his daughters, Sissy and Florence, who lived in Austin. He enjoyed playing golf and puttering around in a golf cart. Hite had just started writing a book about his advertising experiences, and at Lakeway he had time to write and reflect with few interruptions.

Organizing materials for a biography gave Morris a headstart on some lectures he planned to give at UT-Dallas. The university had appointed Morris an adjunct professor in May 1982. First the Dallas bond election and then other commitments had kept Hite out of the classroom, but Dr. Randall Schultz had booked Morris to speak to his UTD marketing classes in early May.

Hite confessed to Caroline that being named an adjunct professor ranked as one of the highlights of his life. His experiences with the Account Executive's Training School at Tracy-Locke had given him a hint of what the seminar setting must be like. Morris also knew he had plenty to say about the subjects of marketing and advertising and, for that matter, how to succeed in business (by really trying).

Back in Dallas on April 23, 1983, the Dallas Press Club saluted Morris' contributions to the city by naming him "Headliner of the Year" at the annual Gridiron show. The Press Club jury pointed to Hite's leadership in the '82 bond election as but one example of an extended effort to make Dallas a better city for all its residents. Hite accepted the Headliner award with his hands hooked inside the belt loops of his tuxedo pants and with the observation that the code of doing business in Dallas often meant "putting city above self."

Just a week later, he would be back in the headlines. Tragically.

Morris Hite awoke early on the morning of Sunday, May 1, 1983. He slipped out of bed and slipped on his Byron Nelson Golf Classic attire. Red trousers. White golf shirt bearing the Salesmanship Club logo. Red ball cap. He sat with Caroline in the kitchen, sipping coffee and going over plans for the day. They agreed to meet for lunch at the main pavilion.

Around 6:30 a.m., Morris kissed Caroline good-bye and climbed into his 1980 Cadillac Seville. He drove westward on Royal Lane toward the new Las Colinas Sports Club in Irving. He crossed under Stemmons Freeway, proceeded past the L.B. Houston public golf course and the new Dallas Communications Complex that builder Trammell Crow hoped would attract the film business to Texas.

When he reached the intersection of Royal Lane and MacArthur Blvd., Hite turned south. One of the main thoroughfares of the city of Irving, MacArthur bisected the Las Colinas property as it ran north into the western extension of Loop 635.

Hite headed toward an early morning rendezvous of Salesmanship Club members called, graphically enough, the Phlegm-Cutter. The Phlegm-Cutter had become a tradition before the tournament's final round. Salesmanship Club members would belt down shots of whisky and toast themselves by saying: "We've had a good tournament so far. Let's don't screw anything up."

Maybe Morris' mind raced ahead to later that afternoon. As Salesmanship Club president, he would be part of the official awards ceremony.

Maybe he was going over a checklist of things to get done that day. Like visit with the CBS-TV officials and the major corporate sponsors. Frito-Lay especially.

Or maybe Morris mulled over a new advertising idea for an Allcom client. He always said the best *idea-hunting* came behind the wheel.

At 6:50 a.m., Hite approached the intersection of MacArthur Boulevard and State Highway 114. The highway ran past the north entrance to Dallas-Fort Worth Regional Airport into Grapevine, Texas.

To help the flow of traffic into Las Colinas for the Nelson Classic, highway officials had put up a temporary stoplight on Highway 114 to give traffic on MacArthur a chance across. What someone failed to consider is that anyone driving down a state highway at 55 mph (or faster) isn't expecting to see a stoplight. The intersection was an accident waiting to happen. And Morris Hite got there first.

As he reached the intersection, the temporary traffic light showed green, and Hite drove ahead. He failed to see on his left a Pontiac heading up Highway 114, the driver oblivious to the stoplight. Morris had trouble turning his stiff neck in that direction, anyway, so maybe he never even saw what hit him.

As Hite moved into the intersection, the Pontiac rammed into the Cadillac broadside behind the driver's seat. The impact threw Morris, who hadn't fastened his safety belt (the mandatory seat belt law not being in effect in 1983), out the door and onto the pavement. He instantly suffered massive head injuries. By the time paramedics arrived at the scene, efforts to revive him proved futile.

Morris Hite lay dead.

The news of the traffic accident dampened many spirits at the golf tournament that day. Native Texan Ben Crenshaw won the 1983 Nelson Classic, then joined the throng around the 18th green in a tearful moment of silence in memory of a dear friend. "Morris Hite and the Morris Hite family are the type people who make Dallas a great city," said Crenshaw. "I'm so proud to win in this city."

Hite's death made the 10 o'clock newscasts, as TV anchormen noted his impact on the city. Dallas newspapers echoed the same sentiments in their Monday morning editions.

Noted *The Dallas Morning News*:. "When the City of Dallas defied tough economic times by trying to win voter approval of a $247 million bond issue last summer, the national news media sent reporters here to record the gloomy election results. They apparently had never met Morris Hite. Hite, the 72-year-old former president of Tracy-

Locke advertising agency, was a man who could take on such apparently insurmountable tasks as chairmanship of the city's bond program and win. The death of Hite in a traffic accident Sunday morning has taken away one of the true 'can do' people of this community, a man who worked tirelessly to help make Dallas the great city that it is. The loss of Morris Hite is an irreplaceable one for Dallas."

Chimed in the *Dallas Times Herald*: "The death of civic leader Morris Hite in an automobile accident Sunday morning is a tragic loss for Dallas. Last year, in what may have been the highlight of his long career of public service, he served as chairman of the city's successful $247 million bond campaign. We join Morris Hite's many friends and associates in mourning his death. We admired him as one of the city's finest leaders and we knew him as an outgoing, generous and thoughtful individual."

Clients, of course, shared the grief. "I feel a strong sense of personal loss because Morris was a close friend as well as a business associate," said Imperial Sugar's Ken Laird. "I've never known anyone that met Morris Hite who didn't like him from the very start. He was warm and friendly and never acted like he was more important than the person to whom he was talking."

A grief-stricken overflow crowd attended a Tuesday, May 3 memorial service at St. Luke's Episcopal Church in Dallas and heard Morris eulogized as a man who worked for progress and for change. A man always ready for the next adventure. "I think more about what's going to happen tomorrow or next year than I do about last year or 10 or 20 years ago," Hite always insisted.

Later that afternoon, following a private service, Morris was buried at Restland Memorial Park.

On the Monday, May 9, 1983, *ADWEEK/Southwest*, an industry news magazine, paid special tribute to Morris Hite.

"Hite will be remembered long and well for such intangibles as the ability to lead, inspire and command respect. In a profession perhaps better known for its characters, Hite had character. Those who worked with or for the Oklahoma native during his 45-plus years in Dallas advertising will, seemingly to the last person, tell you they are better people for the experience."

Those words were among the first I ever wrote about Morris Hite. I'm glad they weren't the last.

CHAPTER NINETEEN

"ADVERTISING IS SALESMANSHIP MASS PRODUCED."—MORRIS HITE

For the men and women who worked with him at Tracy-Locke Co. and Allcom, for his clients and business associates, Morris Hite remains alive. The traffic fatality removed his physical presence on earth, but his spirit stays with them. He deeply influenced and touched every life he entered.

Hite's words remain alive as well:

"Nothing will drive a bad product off the market more quickly than a good advertising campaign. In the final analysis, the best jury to determine the quality and value of any product are the millions of consumers who make the price-value judgment before they buy. Very few products can survive on a one-time sale. Usually the first sale is made at a loss. It is only through repeat business that profits are made. No amount of advertising will convince anyone that a bad product is a good product after they have had a chance to try it one time. American advertisers know this. Consequently, they spend millions of dollars in product and market research before they take a product to market."

"Ethics in advertising? Advertising is about as ethical as the American public. About as ethical as you and your neighbors. About as selfish as you and your acquaintances. It has about the same moral standards as the upper socioeconomic strata of society because it is created, approved and paid for by the upper echelons of modern U.S. society.

"I'll modify that to say that it is a little more ethical, a little more moral, than the upper economic strata of society. Why? Because advertising lives in a fish bowl. It is the most visible of all commercial practices. It has 200 million critics. And no business, no communications medium, no art form (or whatever you want to call advertising), no other enterprise has so many watchdogs."

"A recent case which went before the National Advertising Review Board concerned advertising by the dairy industry in California. Their advertising made the claim that milk has nutritive value. The complaint was that the ads indicated the benefits of drinking milk were obtained immediately rather than after a long period of milk drinking. This is the type of nitpicking complaint that comes frequently from quasi-professional consumer groups.

Nevertheless, it impacts on our business. We are the national advertising agency for the Borden Co. and we prepare advertising on milk. Every line of advertising copy written for Borden—and this is true of virtually all the copy we write—is written with the lawyers figuratively looking over our shoulder. All the copy must be cleared by legal. Now we can't say that milk is good for you. Sometime ago we were told we couldn't say that ice cream is made from cream. The whole thing has become ridiculous. At one time our creative people had a sign in one of the offices that said, *"The legal department says it is unlawful to sell anything to anybody at any price."*

"There have been many objections to advertisements which feature deodorants, laxatives, feminine hygiene products and this kind of thing. However, I believe this falls into the category of good taste rather than ethics. Television, unlike death and taxes, is not unavoidable. If your sensitivities are too badly bruised by watching the tube, there is a simple remedy. Don't watch."

"It takes good clients to make a good advertising agency. Regardless of how much talent an ad agency may have, it is ineffective without good products and services to advertise. Tracy-Locke Co. is fortunate to have good clients who produce products and services that *respond* to good advertising. And it takes *good* products to make good advertising succeed. Unless the product is right, the best advertising in the world will not build a lasting sales success."

"Advertising remains a business of ideas. And ideas are not related to geography. A man with imagination and perseverance is just as apt to come up with a successful sales and advertising idea while working at a desk in San Francisco, Seattle, Portland, Phoenix, Albuquerque or even Dallas, Texas, as he is on Madison Avenue."

"Public relations is not publicity, propaganda, product promotion, press agentry or institutional advertising. And, though these are components or tools, in this case the whole is not equal to the sum of the parts. All these added together are still tools of public relations but not the equivalent.

Public relations is basically three C's—common sense, common courtesy and common decency. With a fourth C—communication. Perhaps a working definition would be *planned persuasive communication designed to influence significant publics.*"

"To establish a favorable and well-defined brand personality with the consumer the advertiser must be *consistent*. You can't use a comic approach today and a scientist in a white jacket tomorrow without diffusing and damaging your brand personality. Being consistent is not as easy as it may sound. Consistency makes it necessary to discard many good advertising and packaging ideas because they do not fit your *predetermined* brand personality.

"The day the Baird family went in the wholesale baking business and decided to name their brand Mrs Baird's Bread, the framework for their brand personality was fairly well defined. The logical brand personality to be projected in advertising ad packaging was that of the dedicated homemaker whose first concern was for her family. From the very beginning the advertising and packaging has attempted to project a warm and friendly feeling plus an atmosphere of trustworthiness and dependability.

"Throughout the years Mrs Baird's advertising has been consistent. It has been clean and uncluttered to connote freshness. Copy has been simple and direct to connote honesty and trustworthiness. It never contains unbelievable claims. It is devoid of gimmickry. Such claims attract new tryers only to disappoint them when they taste no discernible difference as a result of the supposed innovations described in the advertising."

"Advertising is salesmanship mass-produced. No one would bother to use advertising if he could talk to all his prospects face-to-face. But he can't. In Dallas-Fort Worth, it would take 25 salesman making 20 calls a day for 7 days a week *over five years* to cover the market on a single call. And we know that 80 percent of all sales are made after the fifth call.

The United States has become great through mass

production. To sell mass-produced merchandise to millions of people, it became necessary to mass-produce salesmanship. The result was advertising. Through advertising it is possible to call on 75 to 80 percent of your prospects within a matter of days. Through advertising it is even possible to impress your basic sales appeal upon the public so that 60 to 65 percent of them will subconsciously memorize your message. With saturation techniques, this can be done within 60 to 90 days.

"If we will always remember that advertising is salesmanship multiplied, we will not to too far astray. There is no better way to check a television commercial, a radio commercial, a piece of newspaper or magazine copy than to read it aloud and ask yourself: *Does this sound like a well-informed salesman?*

"There is no such thing as national advertising. All advertising is local and personal. It's one man or woman reading one newspaper in the kitchen or watching TV in the den."

"What sort of person succeeds in advertising? Someone who enjoys solving problems. Someone interested in people and things. Someone who is sales-minded.

If you have imagination and the patience to solve problems, it is a good business for you—and you are needed in the business. But it's a tough business which offers little security unless you are *good.*"

"There is more money wasted in advertising by underspending than by overspending. Years ago someone said that underspending in advertising is like buying a ticket halfway to Europe. You've spent your money but you never get there."

"One of our clients, Imperial Sugar Co., recently received a letter from an irate housewife who said: 'I am getting awfully tired of hearing that little girl say 'Imperial Pure Cane Sugar' on television. She is probably some Hollywood brat you paid $10,000 to make the announcement. If you would stop all that expensive advertising and cut the price of your sugar about 10 cents a sack, you might be surprised at how much you would sell.'

"Our client referred the letter to us for reply. We have always believed that unless you get a few letters like this from crackpots your advertising is not getting through. Actually, the client had received a lot of fan mail on the commercial because the little girl, a Dallas youngster who received very modest pay for her work, was wonderfully appealing on TV.

"In our reply we told the lady how happy we were for the opportunity of giving her factual information on the amount of money spent for advertising Imperial Pure Cane Sugar. If we eliminated all advertising for Imperial Sugar and were able to pass on the entire savings to the consumer, the company could reduce the price of sugar by five cents on every 100 pounds. This means the housewife would save on her 5-pound purchase about one-quarter of a cent. And since the grocer does not deal in units of less than one penny, the actual difference probably would end up in increased margin to the grocer and in no savings whatever to the housewife.

"Furthermore, we pointed out that the effectiveness of Imperial Sugar advertising in the region within which it is sold has enabled them to dominate the market and consequently keep sugar prices at a level which averages about 10 cents to 15 cents per 100 wt. lower than most other parts of the country."

"Techniques of art, layout, typography, radio and television productions and fine writing are important. Nevertheless, they are *secondary* to the basic selling proposition around which the ad or commercial is built.

"It is not the purpose of the ad or commercial to make the reader or listener say 'My, what a clever ad.' It is the purpose of advertising to make the reader or listener say, 'I believe I'll buy one when I'm shopping tomorrow,' or 'I wonder if Joe could get one for me wholesale?'

"The place to start in advertising is with a basic selling appeal. An appeal that fulfills some existing need in the prospect's mind, an appeal that can be readily understood and believed."

"Repetition is necessary in advertising. Few people devote their full attention to an ad or commercial. Only after they have seen or heard the same ad or commercial several times do they receive its full impact. Maxwell House Instant Coffee, one of the most successful food specialties of recent years, ran the same ad, "Amazing Coffee Discovery," *for six years* without changing copy."

"I am not saying that good writing and good art direction and good production are not important. But I have said that good thinking—repeat, good thinking—is more important than the best art direction and the very finest writing. The idea *must* come first.

And I am saying that in advertising there are more good art directors and writers than good advertising thinkers. Too many advertising artists and writers depend on technique to cover up for a paucity of ideas."

"Humor is one of the most difficult things to achieve in a 30-second television spot. Every writer thinks he can write humor. Many can, but *few* can do it in 30 seconds. And *nothing* is worse than a spot that is supposed to be funny and isn't."

"A good marketing man is a nosey so and so. He has an irrepressible desire to poke into everything. Especially products and people—what makes them tick. He is an inveterate browser, shopper, sightseer—always on the prowl for something new, different, unusual, rare and, hopefully, exploitable."

"Psychographics frequently are more important than demographics in pinpointing the target market group. We learn through research who represents our most receptive market then talk to them with words and pictures that relate to them as individuals."

"Is advertising moral? It is part and parcel of the American free enterprise system. . . . I challenge anybody to show any [economic] system that has done as much for so many in so short a time."

"A committee consists of a group of men who keep minutes and waste hours."

"There are too many jingles that cannot be understood. I really suffer for the poor advertisers who are paying good money for radio on which the sound is so bad that no one except the man who pays the bill knows what product was advertised."

"If all advertisers used our "How Much, How Good" measurement, many would be shocked to learn how few people have the *vaquest idea* of what they are saying in their advertising. If people don't know what you are saying, there is little likelihood that you will influence them to any great degree."